T0310029

Business Hack

Business Hack

THE WEALTH DRAGON WAY TO BUILD A SUCCESSFUL BUSINESS IN THE DIGITAL AGE

John Lee

This edition first published 2019
© 2019 John Lee

Registered office
John Wiley & Sons Ltd, The Atrium, Southern Gate, Chichester, West Sussex, PO19 8SQ,
United Kingdom

For details of our global editorial offices, for customer services and for information about
how to apply for permission to reuse the copyright material in this book please see our
website at www.wiley.com.

Wiley publishes in a variety of print and electronic formats and by print-on-demand. Some
material included with standard print versions of this book may not be included in e-books or
in print-on-demand. If this book refers to media such as a CD or DVD that is not included in
the version you purchased, you may download this material at http://booksupport.wiley
.com. For more information about Wiley products, visit www.wiley.com.

Library of Congress Cataloging-in-Publication Data

Names: Lee, John, 1981- author.
Title: Business hack : the wealth dragon way to build a successful business
   in the digital age / John Lee.
Description: First Edition. | Hoboken : Wiley, 2019. | Includes index. |
   Identifiers: LCCN 2018039792 (print) | LCCN 2018048897 (ebook) | ISBN
   9781119542308 (Adobe PDF) | ISBN 9781119542315 (Epub) | ISBN 9781119542292
   (paperback)
Subjects: LCSH: Internet marketing. | Selling. | Success in business. |
   BISAC: BUSINESS & ECONOMICS / Finance.
Classification: LCC HF5415.1265 (ebook) | LCC HF5415.1265 .L44 2019 (print) |
   DDC 658.8/72—dc23
LC record available at https://lccn.loc.gov/2018039792

Cover Design: Wiley
Cover Image: ©rudall30/Shutterstock

Set in 11/13pt, NewBaskervilleStd-Roman by SPi Global, Chennai, India

Printed in Great Britain by TJ International Ltd, Padstow, Cornwall, UK

For Mum,
my original "why".

And for Keira,
my new "why".

Nothing is impossible; the word itself says, "I'm possible" …

Audrey Hepburn

Contents

Preface

Imagining a world without the Internet is becoming increasingly difficult. The younger generations have never known a world without the availability of instant online information and resources at the touch of a button. Whether you like it or not, business is conducted in cyberspace. Even the most hands-on, tangible products need to be visible and available to purchase online. We receive the majority of our information through the digital medium, and increasingly not even through our laptops, but through our smartphones and tablets. And yet I still come across people with businesses who are not using all the online resources available to them, who feel reluctant to explore cyberspace, who resist investing time and money in their online presence. I try to impress upon them that the days when using Internet tools for business was optional are long gone; having an online presence, a digital business profile, is now an essential, core element of your business. If you are not online, you are very much offline ... i.e. not in the picture! You and your business exist in today's oversaturated, ultracompetitive business environment. If you have a growing business and you do not have an online presence and a digital marketing strategy, you are virtually lifeless.

I am part of a generation that has watched the Internet come into existence. As I grew up and evolved into an entrepreneur, so the Internet has become a core part of my personal life and my professional world. One of my first jobs was selling domains to business owners who barely knew what the Internet was. I have grown all my businesses by making use of the very latest online resources. I have always loved passing on my knowledge to others, and I get huge satisfaction from watching people learn new skills that help them improve and grow their businesses. In this book

I share with you all my knowledge about using online resources for business growth. Whether you are a fledgling start-up enterprise or a well-established business, I hope you find something useful within these pages. And I look forward to hearing about your success!

John Lee,
October 2018

Acknowledgments

My sincere thanks to everyone who helped bring this book to life. Firstly, my thanks to the John Wiley & Sons team, in particular Gladys Ganaden, Banurekha Venkatesan and Elisha Benjamin. My deepest gratitude also goes to everyone at Wealth Dragons PLC, especially Marcos Souto, Diane Saint and our hard-working events team, without whom Wealth Dragons could not have grown as vibrantly and successfully as it has. And I acknowledge and thank our many speakers and business partners, who have contributed to a fascinating and exciting business journey. To my friends and family, who have watched my adventures in business and have offered endless support in so many ways, I am indebted to you all. I must, of course, thank my beautiful, intelligent and compassionate wife, Jen, who teaches me more about life every day. My business partner, Vincent Wong, is my brother and mentor, and I thank him for guiding and inspiring me for so many years. But most of all, I thank all my students, indeed everyone who comes to our events and joins our programmes. Without you I would know and understand far less about business than I do. Through you, by listening to you and watching you learn, I grow myself. Helping people change their lives for the better is why I do what I do.

About the Author

John Lee is the co-founder and CEO of Wealth Dragons PLC. John founded Wealth Dragons in 2009 with business partner Vincent Wong and the company grew rapidly to become a global leader in promoting events and training programmes that give people the tools to change their lives through creating asset-based wealth and passive income. Recently, John launched Wealth Dragons Online, which is set to become one of the largest e-learning platforms for entrepreneurs in the world.

After a humble start in life, born to Chinese immigrant parents in the north of England, John went from working shifts in his parents' Chinese takeaway business to becoming a self-made millionaire by the time he was 27. Initially creating his wealth by investing in a successful property portfolio, John went on to become an internationally-recognised public speaker, sharing stages with some of the greatest minds of our time, including former US President Bill Clinton, Alan Sugar, Richard Branson, Jack Welch (ex-CEO of GE) and Randi Zuckerberg. By 2018, John had gained over two million followers on his Facebook page and had been featured in the mainstream media, in publications including The Sunday Times, The Huffington Post and The Wall Street Journal, and on the BBC. In 2017, John Lee was awarded "Man of the Year" at the Global Woman Awards.

Business Hack is John Lee's second book published by John Wiley & Sons. He is also the co-author of *The Wealth Dragon Way*, first published in 2015, with its revised edition due out at the end of 2018.

Business Hack

Introduction: My Business Journey

Selling the Future

In 1999, I was sitting in a Media Studies class and my tutor asked me to do some research on a topic – I forget exactly what – in the library. I started complaining about it to one of my classmates and he suggested I use the Internet. I'd vaguely heard of this thing called "the Internet", but I hadn't paid much attention to what it was before this point.

My next stop was the library – not to take out books, but to enquire about using the Internet. I assumed it would be a short cut to doing this laborious research. The topic was something I had absolutely no interest in. In my mind, from what my classmate had told me, I imagined a computer programme that would spew out my research for me, which I could then present to my tutor; it seemed like the best cheating machine ever invented!

The reality, however, was far from that simple.

A librarian showed me how to get online, and pointed out how I could type my key search words into a search engine – probably Yahoo! or MSN. The results looked like an absolute mess to my eyes. This was going to take more time than copying it out of books. I was dyslexic, which made it even harder to scroll through the various results and look for the best information. The unfamiliarity of it all made it excruciatingly frustrating; I couldn't make head nor tail of what I was looking at. I soon gave up and resorted to the books. So much for a short cut; in reality it had cost me precious time!

I hated that first experience of the Internet; I couldn't imagine why anyone would go online to find information!

Cut to almost 20 years later and, like most people, I'm Googling stuff and scrolling through search results countless times a day; effortlessly switching between screen sizes depending on whether I am using my phone, tablet, laptop or desktop. The process of browsing the Internet is so second nature to me that I can have a conversation

1

and watch TV at the *same time* as surfing the net. So can most people I know.

The difference in how we all operate in our lives, between now and less than 20 years ago, is phenomenal. I hardly dare imagine where we will be 20 years from now.

Shortly after my experience of trying to use the Internet to find information for my Media Studies class, I found myself working for a company called Touch Communications. I was 18 years old. I had to "cold call" people and then try to sell them domain names for £350. I would call up some phone company in Manchester and say, "Hello, I'm calling to offer you the domain name ManchesterPhones dot com for a great price today … " When they asked why they should buy it when they didn't do any business on the Internet, my pre-prepared script told me to assure them that in a few years everyone would have their businesses online, and that the best domain names would get the most customers, and that people would be shopping online more than in shops.

The irony was that I didn't actually believe a word of it myself. But I still sold a lot of domain names because, as I quickly discovered, I was a natural salesman. I am one of those people who can "sell ice to Eskimos" as the saying goes. *I* didn't need to believe that those customers needed those domains … I simply had to make *them* believe it.

"If you don't buy it, your competitor will," was one of the most effective lines I used.

Back in those days, people had a fair point when they argued that no one would ever go online when they could simply walk into a shop or pick up the phone. The Internet was slow and unreliable. We weren't even using broadband at that point; we only had dial-up connection. These days, fibre-optic cables ensure that information is at our fingertips in the blink of an eye. When our connection slows down we all get extremely frustrated.

"In ten years, everyone's going to be online, everyone's going to be using the Internet to do their business, socialise and shop," I would say, without believing a word of it. Knowing what I know now, I obviously wish I'd bought up all those domain names myself. I'd have made a killing!

> In ten years from now, everyone's going to be online, everyone's going to be using the Internet to do their business, socialise and shop.
> (My sales script. circa 1999)

From a Northern Town

I was born and raised in Colne, a small town in Yorkshire, England, where my Hong-Kong-born parents owned and ran – with the help of extended family members – the local Chinese takeaway. Growing up in the north of England in the 1980s, when I was literally the only Chinese kid in the school, was tough at times. I got teased and bullied for my ethnicity in a way that is completely unacceptable these days but was sort of tolerated by general British society back then. My family also received a fair amount of abuse from racist people within the local community, but my parents never let it stop them working hard at their business, and they instilled a strong work ethic in me.

During my childhood, watching my family work long hours to keep the business going, I was resentful that I hardly saw my parents, but as I got older I began to appreciate the sacrifices they'd made for me. They were very proud of the Chinese takeaway business that they built and they expected my older brother and me to take over the family business when we left school, as was common in our culture … but I had other plans.

As soon as I was old enough (and even before that) I worked hard at whatever I could find in order to make pocket money at first and then money to support myself through college. At one point I remember I was working in three different jobs at the same time. As well as selling those domain names in the telesales job that I mentioned above, I was also working in a shoe shop at weekends and doing regular evening shifts in my parents' Chinese takeaway. I went through some lonely years in my late teens, when I had no time to socialise and build friendships, but I was determined to follow my own path rather than simply fall into the family business.

One of my strongest motivations was my desire *not* to work the kind of hours I'd seen my parents working. My attitude was, "What kind of life is it if you never get to see your children, or venture out and explore the world?" I wanted time to have new experiences, and money to give me the freedom to travel. I wanted to make sure my future children had more options than I had had while growing up. I also wanted to help my parents out financially, so that they could take more time off; it hurt me to see them working long hours for days on end. I wanted to thank them for all the sacrifices they'd made for me. I was sure that, if I could earn decent money, I could make life much easier for them.

I got the A level grades to get me into the University of Hull to study Animation. I loved every minute of my degree, graduated with a first and got a great job as soon as I graduated. The studio that hired me was in Guildford and I was enthusiastic about moving down south and getting myself closer to London, which was where I hoped I would finally end up.

A year or so later, I got my dream job, at Framestore in central London. Although I was initially excited by the prospect of the considerable pay rise I'd be getting, I soon realised that, once I factored in the rise in my living expenses (I was still living in Guildford but commuting into central London and socialising more), I wasn't really any better off. Finally it dawned on me that I was working all the hours I could fit into a day just to be able to afford to live a fairly modest life. Furthermore, all my efforts went into building someone *else*'s business. I remember thinking to myself, if I'm giving up all my time just to make enough money to live on, how am I any different from my parents? That feeling really inspired my next move.

Into the Property Business

One of my friends at Framestore had started looking at property investing as a way of making an additional income. He gave me the book that had inspired him. Even though I find reading hard because I'm dyslexic, I found couldn't put this book down. I read it with great interest and became fascinated with the idea that I could make a passive income through investing in property. What got me so excited was the concept of "buying back my time", i.e. creating a source of income that gave me enough to live on so I could pursue other interests and business ideas.

I immediately began going to as many property seminars and networking events as I could find. I was determined to get a foothold on the property ladder and start building a portfolio. To keep me on my toes, I actually resigned from my job just before I bought my first property. This gave me a small window in which I could still use my salary to qualify for a mortgage.

I know it sounds rather risky, but I quit my job because I wanted to put the pressure on myself, I wanted to ensure that I couldn't chicken out. In fact, I went "all in", selling my car, borrowing some money from a family member, and generally doing anything and everything I could to put together the money to pay for my new venture.

I found a great mortgage broker and asked him to mentor me. He was expensive but worth every penny as he showed me a way to buy a BMV (Below Market Value) property that would enable me to start my portfolio with very little money down. This was in 2005, before the crash, when mortgages were much easier to get.

The fee I had to pay my mentor was a scary amount, and handing over all that money was painful, but I knew the pain of *not* having the freedom I craved was greater. I never wanted to go back to being an employee. I wanted to be in control of how I spent my time for the rest of my life. That deep desire for ultimate control over how I spent my time helped motivate me for years to come.

With guidance from my mentor, I found a property valued at £250,000 and managed to negotiate a significant discount with the owner. I bought the property for just £200,000, which I financed through a bridging loan. Then, as soon as the property was mine, I refinanced it, taking out a mortgage of £212,500 (i.e. 85% of the official valuation). This was a relatively quick and simple process at the time. In those days, lenders were falling over themselves to offer mortgages to anyone, regardless of their means to pay it back. I paid off the £200,000 bridging loan and had £12,500 left over. After paying off my costs and a small amount of interest on the short-term bridging loan, I had around £9,000 left.

I had been pretty terrified of going into my first deal, but it paid off and I never looked back.

Once I got going, I found myself on a roll. I found out that there were property networking events, so I started going to them, talking to everyone and anyone I could meet. I soon found myself flipping deals, doing joint ventures, making new contacts and building my portfolio. As I got deeper and deeper into the business of property investment, I started to join online forums and other networking groups. It wasn't long before I decided that I wanted to start my own group and mentor people myself.

My path in the property business was all about playing the numbers game. I sought out as many leads as possible, looking for people who wanted to make a quick, secure sale and who were willing to sell properties to me at below market value in exchange for a guaranteed fast sale. That was my business model.

The only problem with this business model was that it was very time-consuming. Yet again I found I was working all hours of the day to keep my business going. This was exactly what I had set out to avoid. I became tired of trudging around the estate agents, begging them to give me leads. They were hard work because they didn't want their clients selling at below market value to me. Estate agents make their money through commissions based on the actual sale price of the property, so it's obviously in their interest to push the price up. Dealing with estate agents was always an uphill battle and I began to look for ways in which I could bypass the estate agents. That's when I discovered that people were actually using the Internet to sell their houses after failing to get any offers by using estate agents. These were people who needed to sell urgently, and were willing to lower the sale price in exchange for a fast, guaranteed sale. I was sure that, if I could find a way for these motivated property owners to find *me*, instead of me always going looking for *them*, I could massively increase the numbers of leads I was getting. So I began researching how to set up a website. This was around the end of 2005.

My First Website

My very first website was called "CompleteIn28Days.com" because my key selling point was that I could guarantee completion in 28 days. I was actively looking for motivated sellers; that was the area of the market I was specifically interested in. In other words, **I knew my market**. This is one of the most important aspects of any successful business, and one that many people don't get right. In actual fact, the Internet had *shown* me my market. When I saw how many people were desperately trying to *sell* their houses online, I could see how many customers I could potentially have if I positioned myself as someone looking to *buy* houses online.

But I wanted to be in business alone this time.

In my early days as a property investor, I had got into business with a guy who offered to build a property portfolio with me. Our deal was that we would share everything equally. We bought 35 houses in six months, mainly thanks to his website funnelling potential leads to me that I would then negotiate. He was the lead generator and I was the dealmaker or "closer". I would call up the leads and try to make a deal. It was a numbers game; I knew if I kept speaking to leads, I would eventually get deals. We were extremely successful.

Unfortunately I hadn't protected myself adequately and my so-called partner was able to renege on our agreement, forcing me to sign over the entire portfolio to him when I had done all that hard work. I lost everything … *except my experience*! Okay, he got the properties, but because I was the one who had made all the deals, I had developed excellent negotiating skills, and no one could take those skills away from me.

I was devastated to lose so much money, but I was also confident that, using my experience, I could build up my own portfolio. The only thing I needed was a way of getting more leads. This was what ultimately motivated me to build a website.

I spent hours and days and weeks researching websites and information about online marketing. I wanted to replicate everything my ex-business partner had provided for me in lead generation. I quickly understood that I needed to build a website as soon as possible and then use Google ads to drive traffic to it.

Around the time I started looking into building websites, a guy called Robert Clark contacted me. He was generating leads but needed someone to close the deals. He had heard of my reputation as a dealmaker and wanted to go into business with me. After my previous experience I was gun-shy, this wasn't what I was looking for, but I *was* curious to know how he got his leads. He showed me his website that he'd built based on the training he'd received from Perry Marshall, a real expert in websites in the early days. Robert told me he'd been on a course and received one-on-one tuition with Perry. He'd been to the US to study with him. The course cost £5,000. So I had a choice; either I could spend £5,000 on the training myself, or I could go into business with someone who had already done it.

Once I made sure that the deal was watertight and I couldn't get screwed over like I was the time before, I decided to go into business with Robert. I did, however, ask for a slightly different deal that wasn't what I originally had in mind. Basically, rather than sharing in the portfolio, I said I'd pay him for any lead he brought to me. I offered him £25 for every lead he brought me, whether it led to a sale or not. I did this for six months. Some of the leads converted to sales and some didn't, but I had to pay Robert for every lead regardless. This meant if he brought me 50 leads in one week, I had to pay him £1,250, even if I didn't make a penny from them. This wasn't the best business model but it showed me how effective Robert's lead generation machine was. I knew I had to find a way of getting those leads myself. I needed to find a way of capturing the traffic he was harnessing. I had to build my own website and figure out how to drive traffic to it.

> ... either I could spend £5,000 on the training myself, or I could go into business with someone who had already done it.

Finally, I reached out to my Uncle James, who was a web designer for a big company. He gave me a book on how to use Dreamweaver, one of the early website-building computer programmes. I remember flicking through the book and being astonished that it was made up of about 600 pages – the longest book I'd even seen! Every night I pored over the instructions, trying to teach myself website construction. If you're familiar with today's hosting and building platforms such as WordPress or Squarespace, you'll know how easy it is to create a decent website these days … you can literally do it in a matter of hours. Next time you're frustrated because it takes you half an hour to redesign a page you lost on WordPress, just think of me back in 2006 spending *three months* reading a massive book, trying to learn how to write code from it, going back and forth over different designs, and agonising over how to repair bugs!

And I didn't even succeed!

After nearly four months of trying, I ditched my efforts and paid someone else to do it for me. I paid them £700, which was a huge sum of money to me back then, but that secured me a functioning website and marked the birth of CompleteIn28Days.com, which served me well for several years.

I was lucky to start building my website when I did, because I was all set up to catch the wave following the global financial crash of 2007–2008, which led to people becoming increasingly desperate to sell their houses. I always reference this when I want to prove the point that a recession can be a great time to make money if you look for the right market. I urge people not to panic in a recession; there is plenty of money to be made, especially for individuals and small businesses, if you can catch the right market. My key market included the people who needed to sell their properties before getting into negative equity. I was offering a quick, secure sale to people who needed to sell urgently in order to avoid going into debt. My market was not made up of people who could afford to hold out for the best price for their properties; my market was made up of people who needed to sell in 28 days and be relieved of their financial burden.

Most business owners have no idea how many potential new customers they have out there in the world. I can't say the following enough times …

There are people sitting by their computers right now, with their credit cards to hand, who are eager to buy what you are selling. You just haven't found them yet, and they don't know how to find you.

But they are there. If you make it easy for them to find you, with the right website and effective marketing tools, you will not stop making money.

If you have a product that people need and want, your ideal market is out there somewhere, I guarantee you. And the Internet can take you to it, instantly. *You don't even know how big your market is yet!*

The Importance of Marketing

Going back to that time I described above, when I first launched my website … as soon as I had my website up and running, I was sure it was only a matter of time before I started generating thousands of leads.

But that isn't what happened.

Why? Because I wasn't doing the right marketing. There's no point in having an attractive shop front if no one is walking by. Whatever you create, you still have to show it to people, to tell them that the product exists; people still need to be informed. I could finish writing this book and it would be an accomplishment, but I won't make any money from it until it is published *and* marketed. Even once it is published, it has to be marketed so that people *know* about it. Otherwise how can they buy it?

You're not going to make a dime until people **know your product exists and are shown the place where they can buy it.** When I finished my first book I thought my job was done, but it had actually only just begun. I always tell people who are about to write a book … you spend about 20% of your time and effort writing the book, and the other 80% selling it.

When I realised I wasn't getting traffic coming to my website, I began to research solutions. Eventually I found an online course for only £100 that promised to teach me all I needed to know about Internet advertising. I bought it and started learning all about marketing online, how to use Google ads and other tools.

Unlike the Dreamweaver book, I got through the course in about a day. It took me a couple of hours to put up my first campaign and within 25 minutes, my first lead came through. I couldn't believe it. The leads kept on coming and I never looked back. I have never forgotten that wonderful feeling, the first evening I realised I'd cracked it; I had figured out how to get potential clients on demand. I had no idea, then, just how powerful a tool I had discovered, not just for my *own* business – for *any* business.

Within a few months I was getting around 200 leads a month. At least five of these turned into deals. So I was either buying or flipping (usually for around a £1,000 fee each time) five or more properties a month. I was on track to complete 60 property deals in my first year.

One of the most remarkable trends I noticed (and I have continued to see this trend throughout my time in business) is that when people find *you*, you can pretty much name your price. They've chosen you already so you don't really have any competition. It was so easy; I couldn't believe it. No more grovelling to estate agents and begging for leads. I finally had potential clients on demand.

There was no way I'd have been in that position, of having clients come to me, without: (a) **having a good website** and (b) **marketing it effectively**.

> … when people find you, you can pretty much name your price. They've chosen you already so you don't really have any competition.

An Online Revolution

I soon had people throughout the property business asking me how I was doing so much business. They wanted to advertise their own businesses like I did, and wanted me to teach them how to do it. They asked me how much I would charge to teach them everything I knew. I said my fee was £1,000 per day. I arrived at this price by thinking about what it would cost me to take a day away from my business and spend it entirely with someone teaching them. I could easily spend a day negotiating a deal worth £1,000, so that was the price I set. I was giving up a whole day when I could have been going through property leads and calling potential sellers; a day when I might have got a sale that I could have flipped for a £1,000 fee, so my time, I believed, was worth at least £1,000 per day. What's more, I found people who were prepared to pay that. All I did was teach people exactly what I'd learned from a £100 online course. I taught 67 clients within about a six-month period.

I earned £67,000 from teaching people what I'd learned from spending £100.

That was some return on investment! And suddenly it occurred to me that, as I seemed to be good at teaching people, I could do *that* as a business and it might be scalable. In that case I would need more potential leads of people who wanted to learn what I could teach.

What occurred to me next was this ... perhaps I could replicate what I'd done with property deals in the field of property *education*. In other words, could I apply all my knowledge and experience of finding leads from house sellers to finding deals from property investors who wanted to learn what I was teaching? How could I find more clients who wanted to learn this stuff for £1,000 per day? I did an online search for "property education" then I looked up "property courses" and then "property mentor". I identified a gap in the market and put up an ad saying, "Are you looking for a property mentor?" and this directed people towards my data capture website. These data capture sites had already proved highly effective for me.

So I would sit at home and my email would ping when someone new entered their details. One by one I would call people and get more information from them. When I reached them on the phone, I'd say, "Hello, this is John Lee, you entered your details onto my website ... what do you want mentoring in specifically?"

A trend soon emerged. People mostly wanted the same things. They all said they wanted to learn "How to find property deals" or "How to negotiate property deals" or "How to get started in property investing". Then they would ask me how much I charged for mentoring. When I said £1,000 per day, many of them would say no, that it was too expensive, but out of 50 leads, on average, one always said yes. And thus I discovered that, whatever price point you place yourself at, someone out there will be willing to pay it; you just have to play the numbers game and go through as many leads as you can, as quickly as possible, in order to get to the "yes" that you need.

My success was remarkable. I had no formal qualifications in property. To the outside world, I was nobody, but within my field I had begun commanding respect because I had become an expert at doing what I was doing. I got results that people could see, and they wanted to learn how to do that, too. I quickly discovered that people are always willing to pay for expert knowledge, for specialised knowledge. If you're a heart surgeon, for example, you're going to get paid more than a GP.

I recently coached a woman who had just finished writing an e-book on refurbishing houses. The book was full of unique business tips that she had learned as she worked her way up through the property business. She asked me how much she should sell her book for. I told her to price it at £97. When she told her son, he balked at this. He asked why someone would pay £97 for her book. I defended my suggestion to her by explaining that she was selling *expert* knowledge, *unique* knowledge, that people could not get anywhere else, *and* knowledge that could help people make a lot of money.

> ... **whatever price point you place yourself at, someone will be willing to pay it.**

Still Trading My Time for Money

It wasn't that long before I was making more money from teaching than from doing property deals. Great, I thought... but in the next moment I realised that it was the same book with a different cover. In other words... I was back to *trading all of my time for money*. This was *still* not what I had hoped to achieve in my business life. I still wanted a good source of passive income. Teaching was incredibly time-intensive and I wanted my time back; after all, that was my primary motivation for wanting to get into the property business in the first place. That's when I had a brainwave. If I could put all the information I was teaching people into something that was tangible, like a physical book or an electronic file, maybe I could sell it as a product. If I put my knowledge into a PDF file and sold it for £100, I would only need to sell 10 copies to make £1,000, which was the sum it was currently taking me a day to make by coaching.

So that's what I did. I created an e-book and sold it online for £100.

From that point on, whenever people contacted me to ask if I could teach them, if they could come to me for mentoring, I simply told them I didn't have time, but that I *could* sell them my teaching notes for £100. And here's the best thing... far *more* people were willing to spend £100 than the 1 out of every 50 or so leads who were willing to pay £1,000 for a day's training, so I had actually found a product for which there was a much bigger market.

Finally, I felt like I had cracked the best business model for making a passive income. Furthermore, it was clearly scalable.

As time marched on, the next big popular thing in the online education market was the training video. People who had read my book started asking if I had any training videos. They had liked what they had read in my e-book, but they wanted more. They wanted to *see* me teaching it to them. By this time, YouTube had really begun to take off and people were keen on "how to" videos.

To meet this obvious and clear demand, I decided to have a go at making some videos of me teaching. I created a website that required people to register and pay a monthly membership fee in exchange for access to all my videos. I set my membership fee at £100, believing that (like with the e-book) many of the people who had originally said no to spending £1,000 on a day's training with me might be willing to pay £100 a month for my knowledge. I sent out an email, with a link to the site, to my database (which stood at around 5,000 email addresses at that time).

In the first 24 hours, 110 people signed up to the website for £100 per month. I made £11,000 in one day. I could hardly believe it. And the uptake continued until I was making more money from my membership site than from my property portfolio.

As time went on, some people naturally cancelled their monthly subscriptions, but they were quickly replaced by new members, and overall the numbers steadily went up. Every time someone made contact with me, to enquire about tutoring, I sent them the details of the membership site. More often than not they signed up for at least a few months.

I kept the business going for about two years until it ran its course, partly because I couldn't compete with all the free tutorials that were being posted on YouTube. But during that time, it really was the true passive income that I'd been looking for.

> **In the first 24 hours, I had 110 people sign up to the website for £100 per month. I made £11,000 in one day.**

The story of how I met my business partner, Vincent Wong, and started Wealth Dragons is told in detail in our first book, *The Wealth*

Dragon Way. Forming and growing Wealth Dragons has been one of the biggest and most exciting adventures of my life, and it is still evolving and growing as I write. When it came to writing a second book, I wanted to share, in more detail, some of the tools and skills I've used to build my business. Specifically, I want to focus on what it takes to build a successful business in the digital age. I wanted to share with you, here in the introduction, my long relationship with the Internet. I have been there from the start, and I have watched online tools launch and evolve. I've tried them all. I've made all the mistakes and discovered exactly how to get the best out of them. And now I want to share all my knowledge with you in order to help you grow your business in an Internet-dependent world!

What's in This Book for You?

The world is changing at an ever-increasing rate and it is exhausting trying to keep up. Nowhere does it change faster than in cyberspace. Indeed, the rapid changes to how the online world operates makes it almost impossible to write a book about all the current trends and available tools, because by the time it's published half the information will be out of date. Nevertheless, there is still enormous value in learning how today's online tools and platforms help your business, and in absorbing the fundamental message I am trying to put across in this book, because it will still help you navigate *tomorrow*'s tools and services. And certain fundamental factors about successful business practices will never change.

The fundamental message of this book is this: **you *cannot* run a successful business today or in the future without a substantial digital footprint, i.e. without having a competitive online presence.** Whether you are a long-established business, a global company, a local establishment, a start-up or a budding entrepreneur with a million ideas, *you need to be online.* You need to be aware of all the online platforms and tools that are available to you, and you need to stay on top of all the changes that are made (these days on an almost daily basis) and new products on offer. Even if you are a small, local restaurant, you need a presence. You need a website at the very least, that is discoverable on Google. But to be taken seriously, you also need a social media presence. If you are a restaurant, for example, you *must* have a Facebook page and an Instagram account in order to post pictures of your food and to build a community of followers (customers and fans). Most businesses also benefit from a Twitter account. If you are a freelancer, or an entrepreneur, you must have a LinkedIn account. Every business will have competitors, and if your competitors are more visible online than you, then they will have an initial advantage when it comes to attracting new business.

Anyone who has a business (no matter what size it is) or plans to build a business will benefit from the knowledge in this book. If you have not yet explored all the opportunities that are available to you via the Internet then I believe that the information I share in this book could help you revolutionise your business.

Today, tomorrow and for the foreseeable future, the Internet is the most powerful channel through which you can communicate with your customers. Ignore it at your peril!

In order to help you understand how and why you have to embrace and use the latest online tools and platforms, in the first part of this book I am going to outline what I call the "old rules". That is not to say that these rules are defunct, just that these are some of the fundamental and traditional building blocks for any business that need to be understood in order to appreciate the importance of the "new rules" that I will set out in the second part of the book. In the third section of the book we will explore the future, discussing ways of staying ahead of the curve and speculating on what kind of technological developments might impact how we operate in the coming years.

In the final part of the book I have shared stories of people who have used my coaching to grow their businesses. I am constantly inspired by the success stories of my students and I hope, one day, to hear *your* success story!

PART I

THE OLD RULES

1

Your Business and Products

What is your business? And what are the fundamental rules associated with building and growing that business? Before we look at how you position your business for success in the digital age, let's look at what your business *is* and go through some of the traditional rules for building any successful business.

What is Your Business?

In fact, before you answer that question let's answer this one. What is *a* business? That's easy, right? *A business sells something.* But you'd be amazed by how many people fail to understand this.

If you are not selling something, or planning to sell something, then you don't have a business. You may have a *brand*, you may have a large *following*, but until you are actually selling a product or service (and ideally for a profit), you don't have an actual **business**.

Interestingly, the digital age has given us the ability to look like a business even when we're not. We can all start a **brand**, by thinking of a name, buying a website, designing a fancy logo, creating social media pages and even getting thousands of people to follow us, but until you are trading a product or service (even if it is your own power of endorsement), you do not have a business. Many so-called "entrepreneurs" or "start-ups" do not fully appreciate this point. Many of them have a **brand** but not a **business**. This is not to say you cannot turn your brand into a business (and we will go into more detail on this subject later in the book), but until you are selling a product or service, you are not really operating as a business.

Whether you have an existing business or are planning to create a business sometime in the future, the most important question you should be asking yourself is not, "How can I make money from a business?" but, **"What do people need?"** The smartest business people don't think in terms of making money, they think in terms of solving problems. If you can identify a big problem that many people have and find a great solution to it, you will automatically make money.

So what do you have that people need? What value can you bring to other people's lives? What can *you* do or make that is better, or more efficient, than anything anyone else is providing?

> **If you can identify a big problem that many people have and find a great solution to it, you will automatically make money.**

A good salesperson knows what people *need*. Have you ever wondered why you sometimes go to the supermarket intending to buy a couple of items you've written on a list, that shouldn't total more than about £25, but instead you come away with a huge shopping bag full of items you hadn't intended to buy and your bank account is £100 lighter?

If you've ever shopped in Ikea, you've probably noticed how you are directed to walk through the "marketplace" before you get to the checkout. Or maybe you never even noticed and wondered how the car doors will hardly close. You only went to Ikea to get a mirror and a couple of chairs, but you left with four bags full to bursting with cushions, vegetable peelers, tea lights, wicker baskets, storage jars, a Tupperware set, placemats, avocado slicers, chopping boards, photo frames, fairy lights, egg cups, candles, clothes hangers, cucumber keepers, banana holders, a few plants, and several stuffed animals! This is because someone has successfully sold you stuff you didn't even know you even needed. But you were in the shop in the first place because you *did* need something. There was something you wanted that took you into a place where you were offered *other* items that you suddenly realised you needed. This is the first rule of selling: first give people what they want… then sell them what they need.

> The first rule of selling: give people what they want ... then sell them what they need.

The Definition of a Business

As I explained above, unless you are selling something – a product or service – you do not have a business. The very definition of a business is an operation that involves the exchange of two things of value. For example, you give me a product that has a value and I give you money that has value. We could also exchange goods – that is a business transaction. You can sell anything: products such as books, computers, phones, cakes, clothing, food and cars, and services such as dog walking, wedding planning, hairdressing, and window cleaning.

My businesses have mostly been service-based, but in the course of my career I have helped countless people find and develop businesses that offer both products and services, so I have a wealth of experience across many different industries and markets. I have helped people with a huge range of different businesses. I've worked with property developers, hoteliers, spa owners, accountants, solicitors, restaurant owners, wedding planners, image consultants, personal trainers, models, hairdressers, educators, child carers, estate agents, writers, singers, and many more. I start by ensuring that they do have a viable business and then I help them tweak their business to ensure that they are selling a product or service that people actually *need*. Finally, I figure out the best way of marketing that product or service, which includes building the most effective digital presence and marketing strategy.

However, before you get your digital presence and marketing right, you *have* to get your product or service right. Having been a mentor and coach to so many different people, across so many different industries, I feel I have become something of an expert at identifying exactly what a person *should* be selling and how best to go about selling it.

Choosing the Right Product or Service

When someone comes to me for help with growing their business, the first thing I do is I look at their business and ask, "What is it you are selling?" Once I know what their existing product or service is, I start asking specific questions to get to the heart of: (a) whether that product or service is the most niche and unique thing that this particular person has to offer, and (b) whether the product or service answers a problem that people have. In other words, how does your product or service solve a problem people have, and how is it different or better than anything anyone else is selling? What is it that you can offer that no one else is currently offering? If we can't find adequate answers to those questions then we need to reassess your business.

It's imperative to work out if there is a difference between what you *are* selling and what you *should* be selling. If you haven't chosen the right product or service to sell in the first place, then no amount of digital marketing will help you. Before you go on to apply the advice in the rest of this book, about building an online following and using all the Internet tools available to you, make sure you are selling the best possible product or service.

I meet so many people who pick a product or service to sell simply because they love it. If you've picked your product or service because *you* like it or need it, this doesn't necessarily guarantee you will be able to sell it. You must ensure that there is a demand for it or you could end up with a lot of unsold inventory sitting around. I've seen this happen. I've also seen people waste a lot of time creating services that no one wants. Yes, you must have passion for a product or service that you want to sell, it has to be something you are able to offer, and preferably something that you would want yourself, but it *must* be something others want and need, too. Always test your market before you invest too much time and money investing in what you *want* to sell; as much as you love it, it might not be something people actually need. In which case, there is no point in producing and marketing it. *You will only be wasting your money.*

I can't tell you how often I make the above (obvious when you read it) point to people and they completely ignore it. Sometimes I think people just get so attached to their ideas that their ego won't let them let go! It makes me so sad to watch people lose money because they can't lose their egos and let go of their passion project once they've discovered there is no market for it. They think they can just create a market. *You can't sell people what they don't want or need!*

Selling Information

A product is not always some kind of gadget or material object; a product can be information, and the digital age has made the process of selling information easier than ever.

Information is potentially one of the most profitable things you can sell because the profit margins can be so high. Remember that e-book I wrote and sold for £100 to every person who bought it? It cost me a couple of days of my time, and then some marketing costs, but it was mostly all profit.

It's easy to underestimate the true value of what you know, but what seems obvious and intuitive to you is often a goldmine of unknown knowledge to someone else, and as long as you can figure out how to package and deliver that information (for which there will be relatively low production costs), you have many ways of maximising the way you generate revenue from it. If I'm selling a physical product (say a T-shirt, a phone or a bicycle), each one costs me an amount of money to make. If I package up information the right way (say as an e-book), my production costs are finished as soon as it's available. After that, each one I sell is, effectively, 100% profit, less some marketing costs. Selling information can be highly lucrative for this reason.

Again, though, let's remind ourselves what a business is and make sure we stay aware that, whatever you are selling, be it a physical, tangible product or electronic information, you only have an *actual* **business** when you are offering a product or service to people at a price that potentially makes you a profit.

Taking your Product to Market

As I've stated above, there is no point in selling a product or service unless you know there is a market for it. So it makes sense to find and know your market, and then create a product for it, rather than create a product you love and then figure out if there is a market for it (Because you may discover there is *no* market for it, which means you've wasted your time and money, and you may – as I've described above – find it much harder to let go of that product once you've fallen in love with it!)

Remember, you must make something that people want and need, otherwise you won't have a business. If you love inventing, become an inventor, but find someone who is going to pay for the research and development that allows you to do this. If you only create what *you* like, without testing your market first, you can only *hope* that someone else will like and buy it.

"Hope" on its own is not a good business plan!

So, if you want a successful business, find out what people need and then create it. Again, remember the key to any successful business is: **give them what they want then sell them what they need.** Just go back to the example I gave earlier about shopping in Ikea to see how this works ... the store **gives** you what you came in for (the sofa, the mirror, the bathroom unit, etc.) and then **sells** you what you **need** (the avocado slicer, the lemon keeper, the storage solutions, etc.)

With all this information in hand, we can break down the process of taking your product to market like this:

1. **Choose your market**

   Obviously it helps if you choose your market according to what your interests are and what most inspires you; this will make the process of finding out what product or service people *need* within that market more interesting. You should definitely try to align your chosen market with your passion. You need everything you can get to keep you motivated, so think carefully about what your greatest passion is. That's a good place to start when you're choosing your market. Even if you already have a business, you should do this exercise because it might be that you are not selling the best product, or that you are not in the right market for *you*. So ask yourself: What holds your interest? What are you particularly good at? Even if your passion isn't immediately obviously to you, you must stay open-minded and observant. Notice what inspires you. Ask your friends and family what they have noticed you are already talking about. Sometimes it's something you've read about that catches your interest and you realise you could really get excited about it. Maybe you have a message to share. Perhaps your message is about health or exercise. This goes back to the question: What is your passion? **Find your passion and let that lead you to your market.**

2. **Find out what your market wants**

   When you've decided which market you would like to be active in, you need to research the needs of your market *in order to find a gap to fill.* There's a simple and free way of doing this. Google has a tool called "Keyword Planner". It's a *free* research tool that will tell you what sort of demand there is for a particular topic. For example, if I was a great singer and wanted to teach people how to sing, I'd try to find out what people want, what they are *searching* for, what they seem to need. Then I can develop the best product or service to sell to them, in order to meet those needs. At the time of writing I have just typed, "learn to sing" into the Google Keyword Planner and I have discovered that 5,400 people in the world typed in "learn to sing" last month. But "learn to sing" is only one variable. If I now type in "how to learn to sing" I am informed that 1,900 typed in these words last month. I can keep going like this, typing in phrases like, "learn to sing online" and "learn how to sing online" or "learn to sing software" and I can keep adding to the total figure. What does this all tell me? It tells me that there is a multitude of people out there in the world who are searching on Google *every month* for ways to learn to sing! So, if I'm passionate about singing, I have found a large market that aligns with my passion. Now I need to develop the best product to market to all those people.

3. **Design the product your market wants**

    Often, your product will become apparent to you through your market research. When I started teaching and giving seminars, I grew passionate about public speaking. I then discovered that there was a huge market for people who wanted to learn public speaking skills, so I perfected my own skills and then taught other people how to do what I was doing. I discovered a market I was passionate about, I found out what people needed (training in public speaking), and then I created products and services that filled those needs. I identified a problem people had – a need to get better at public speaking – and I provided a solution – public speaking training. When you design a product, as well as providing a solution to a problem people have, you also have to figure out the best way to *deliver* that solution. You have to test your product *and* the delivery of it. How do your potential customers want to digest information? For example, I find that some products are best delivered via video, some via audio and some via a live presentation. You must test your market though. **Ultimately, only through testing the product you think your market wants will you find out what they *actually* want.** There is a whole section on testing your market later in the book.

4. **Sell the product to your market**

Once you have chosen your market, identified what people need within that market and designed a product that meets those needs, that provides a solution to their problem – you are ready to sell your product to your market. So now you need to tell people that you and your business exist, by marketing to them, and give them a place to buy your product by driving traffic to your sales site. In today's fast-moving digital age, the tools I outline in the second part of this book will become essential to you when you are ready to take your product to market.

2

Sales and Marketing

Once you've determined *what* you are selling, it's time to focus on the process of selling it, and in order to sell it you have to work out a marketing strategy. Your marketing strategy tells people who you are and what you are selling; your sales strategy gets them to buy it. First of all we are going to look at your **marketing strategy**, at how you provide information to people, and then at the channels through which you sell your products and services. In subsequent chapters we will look more closely at the traditional **sales machine** and **conversion strategies**.

The AIDA Marketing Formula

The best way of getting information to people directly is to send them the information in an email. You need your potential customers to know who you are, what you are selling and how they can get it. The first part of that process is to get them to open an email from you. Once they've opened your email, you need to get them to click through to your website, and finally you need to get them to purchase the product or service you have on offer.

If the first part of the process is getting people to read an email, how do you get someone to *open* an email in the first place? You need to write an enticing headline that gets their **attention** or makes them **aware**. Your headline (written in the subject field of your email) is designed to "sell the open", i.e. to get them to open the email. Next you have to "sell the click", i.e. get them to click through to your website. You do this by writing text in the body of the email that will

interest them enough. Once they have landed on your website, the copy must create the **desire** to take **action** and this will lead them to take up your "call to action"; this might be to sign up for a free course, watch a video or receive a free product. All these things are successful marketing aids as they tell your potential customer about what you are selling; they also educate your customer as to why they need your product or service.

What I have described above is the AIDA marketing formula. Most successful marketing campaigns follow this formula:

A = attention (sometimes also called "awareness")

I = interest

D = desire

A = action

First you get their **attention**, then you hold their **interest**, next you give them the **desire** for the product, and finally you encourage them to take **action** and show them how.

Attention

To get someone's attention you have to shock them, stir their curiosity or ask them a question. Think about what grabs your attention. When you are out on the street, notice the adverts and headlines that grab your attention and if you see something really good don't be afraid to steal it. Someone once said, "good artists copy but great artists steal!"

Interest

Once you've grabbed someone's attention you must hold their interest. To keep them interested you really have to connect with them. What holds your interest in life? You have to keep people reading; you have to make sure they are dying to find out what has happened or what is going to happen. One way to keep their interest is to present a problem and lead them to want to find a solution to that problem. Think through how you can communicate this to them in the body of your email.

Desire

Once you have caught and kept your customer's interest, by connecting with them, you need to stir a desire in them to find out more. If you have presented them with a problem in order to hold their interest, no doubt they will now want to find a solution to that problem. Your next job is to offer them the solution to their problem.

Action

By this point, you have caught someone's attention, held their interest by identifying a problem they have, and created a desire in them to find a solution to the problem, so the next logical step is for them to take the "call to action" that you present them with. Ensure you make it easy for them to take that call to action, whether it is leaving their email address to receive a free gift, or clicking through to your sales site where they can download a free e-book. Make sure that the call to action gives them something.

Basic Sales Techniques

If you've got your marketing right, and you've captured your intended audience, then the next step is to make the sale. No business transaction has taken place until you **make the sale**.

There is a process of basic sales techniques that, if you complete successfully, should more or less guarantee you a sale. At every stage of the process you are selling something. First you sell the **features**, next you sell the **benefits**, then you sell the **scarcity**, then you sell the **social proof**, and finally you sell the **third-party authority**.

1. **Sell the features**

   This is fairly straightforward. Imagine you are selling a phone. Think of all the great features you can describe, such as the high-definition camera, the voice command and the highly durable screen. Imagine you have a dog-walking service. How would you sell the features of your dog-walking service? Maybe the features include taking the dog for a run in a secure, designated dog park, as well as providing healthy doggie treats. Maybe you specialise in dogs of a certain breed that play well together. Whatever you are selling, you must have a list of all the features of your specific product or service.

2. **Sell the benefits**

   How is your product or service going to benefit your customer's life? In the case of the phone, perhaps the high-definition camera will allow your customer to take professional-quality pictures that will, in turn, benefit his or her business. For the dog owner, it will give him or her an extra hour to use in their day, which could enhance their business if they are self-employed. It's always more important to sell what the product will *do*. There's an old saying in sales, **"Don't sell the steak, sell the *sizzle*."** You don't sell the "what" you sell the *why*.

3. **Sell the scarcity**

   You need to show your customer that they will miss out if they do not buy soon. For example, you could explain that you only have two phones left in stock, or only one left at this special price. Or you only have one more space for an additional dog in your dog-walking schedule. Or there are only two tickets at a certain price. Airlines and train companies often use this tactic; they will sell off a certain number of seats at a low price and tell you, when you are considering making a booking, that "there are only two seats left at this price," to encourage you to buy.

4. **Sell the social proof**

   This is your opportunity to show that everyone else is using the product or service and loves it. Show how happy your other customers are with their phones, or show all the recommendations and testimonials you have for your dog-walking service. You are working the psychological angle here. People want to do what everyone else is doing. If you walked into the centre of a town you'd never visited before and you saw that there were two restaurants, one on either side of the road and there is a huge queue outside one and nobody waiting outside the other one, you'd automatically want to go to the more popular one. It's "herd mentality". Watch children follow this pattern time and time again. Most people want to do what "the pack" is doing.

5. **Sell the third-party authority**
    The final stage of the sale is your opportunity to add a "deal closer" that comes from a third-party authority. If you were a sales assistant on a shop floor, you could say, "Let me go and speak to my manager and see if I can get you a 20% discount." You leave the customer wondering whether they are going to get a great deal. They already want the product but if they further believe that they will be getting it cheaper than they'd previously thought, this will probably close the deal. Not only are they attracted by the money they will save, they also feel special, like you've done them a personal favour. (Note: the customer can also use this strategy against you in order to get out of the sale by saying, "I just have to get my spouse to agree before I make the purchase," and then returning to say that their spouse has said "no". They have just used third-party authority to get out of the sale!)

Back to Being a Kid

I couldn't begin to count how many times I have heard people telling me that they "don't know how to sell". I tell them that we are almost born knowing how to sell and it is only as we mature as adults that we lose that ability, mostly because we become self-conscious. If they don't get it, I tell them to think back to when they were a kid. I'm sure we've all had a version of the following exchange (or have seen it recently in kids we know). Picture the scene: Kid asks Dad if he can have a new bike. "It's got the best stuff, Dad," he says, "It has nine gears, reflective stripes and the latest cantilever breaks," (see how he is **selling the features**?) When Dad says no, he goes on to say, "But we're allowed to store them at school, so if I got one I could ride to school and get fit and you wouldn't have to drive me any more" (now he is **selling the benefits** – Kid gets healthy, Dad gets more time in the morning from not having to do the school run). Seeing that Dad's wavering, Kid pushes on with, "And the local bike shop only has *two more* in stock that are on sale, after that they'll go way up in price" (here he is artfully **selling the scarcity**). Dad's unconvinced, so Kid comes up with "But *everyone* at school has one now" (in order to **sell the social proof**) and to close the deal he finishes with: "But *Mum* says I can have one" (thereby **selling the third-party authority**). We all knew how to be expert negotiators when we were kids, we just need to remember our skills and apply them to our "grown-up" toys!

The Deal-Closing Triangle

The most important part of the sales process is, of course, **the close.** I teach my students that there are three phases of closing a deal. When I teach this to a room full of students, I demonstrate it as three corners of a triangle as shown in Figure 2.1, each with a triangle inside because each phase itself has three parts.

1: Make Sure They Like You

You want to deal with people you like, and so do your customers. To get them to like you, make sure you follow three important steps: **introduce** yourself, then get their **attention** and finally get their **permission.** If you can successfully complete these three steps they will like you. Remember:

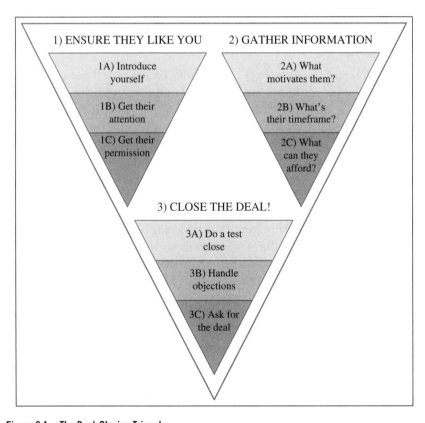

Figure 2.1   The Deal-Closing Triangle

> **People will deal with people they like.**
> **The head won't listen until the heart is engaged.**
> **When you have their attention, you will get their permission.**

Point 1A: Introduce yourself   The most important aspect of your relationship with your potential customers is your rapport with them. People will deal with people they like, so it is essential to build a rapport with them. You can do this very effectively by engaging in a process called "**match and mirror**". Basically, you match and mirror their behaviour. If they smile, you smile; if they are serious, you are serious; if they use foul language, you use foul language. Human beings like to connect, to feel they have something in common with each other. Why do people so often talk about the weather? Because it is common ground. We all know that first impressions are everything, so you must make a great first impression. Think carefully about your clothes. Common sense tells you that you do not go to a business meeting in shorts and a T-shirt. If you do, you are simply not going to be taken seriously. Conversely, you wouldn't go to a football match in a suit and tie. Think about your customers and your surroundings, and dress appropriately. If in doubt, ask advice. For example, if you are invited to a networking event, ask the organisers what is the standard dress code. You should also think about what your customers expect. If I go to a super car meet and I don't have a super car, it's going to look a bit weird. Every time I travel in First Class, everyone is smartly dressed (unless they are a mini-celebrity, in which case they dress in whatever they want). Match and mirror your surroundings.

Point 1B: Get their attention   If you want to get your customer's attention, you must speak to their heart first. There is a saying that "the head won't listen until the heart is engaged". This is why you always have to get to the very *root* of what your customer wants, so you can figure out what they need; this will hook them in. Hooking them in is all about getting their attention. People are always busy. If you want their attention you have to figure out what to say to them to get them to stop what they are doing and give you 100% of their wholehearted attention. You have to be able to stop them in their tracks and literally "hook" them in. The most effective way of doing this is with an elevator pitch, a one-liner, such as: "How would you like to make a 50% return on your investment?" if you are pitching a great business opportunity, or, "How would you like never to work again?" You can keep throwing hooks at them until one works.

Point 1C: Get their permission   In order to build a rapport with someone (which you need in order to go on to the next phases of closing a deal), you must get their permission to keep asking them questions in order to get to know them better. You need to delve quite deeply into what makes them tick (we will cover more of this in a forthcoming chapter that explores the "psychology of selling"). You need to know their problems, their dreams and their desires. You need to know what bothers them and what excites them. You can only do this if you ask questions. But if you don't get their permission, they could be quite defensive, because you could come across as being too intrusive and put them on guard. Basically, ask if you can ask! The more you know about them, the more you can help them, so you need to delve deep in order to discover their needs. But you just need to get their permission before you do this.

> **Match and mirror your customer and surroundings.**
> **Try different statements until you hook your customer's attention.**
> **Get your customer's permission to ask them further questions.**

2: Get the Information You Need

Once you've got your potential customer to like you, and you have permission to ask questions and build a rapport with them, you need more information about them. You must get enough information to make an informed decision on how best to help them. To do this you need to **find out what motivates them**, and then **find out their timeframe**, and finally **find out what they can afford**.

Point 2A: Find out what motivates them   When I am teaching people about making property deals I explain that the biggest mistake is to talk about the house. People aren't passionate about the house they are selling (remember, they are trying to get rid of it); they are passionate about their *reason* for wanting to move … their **motivation**.

It's your job to find out what your potential customer's motivation is. When I'm finding motivated *sellers* (who are my key customers in my property business) I need to find out their reason for moving. Is it because a baby is on the way and they need more space, or they have got a new job starting in a new town in a month's time, or do they need to move closer to their elderly infirm parents? **Find out what is driving their move.** If there isn't an urgent reason, then they are not a motivated seller and, in property, I don't deal with unmotivated sellers. With any potential sale, if you want to have the best chance of closing the deal, you must clearly understand your customer's motivation.

Point 2B: Find out their timeframe   Knowing your customer's timeframe helps you measure their motivation. Indeed, their timeframe *qualifies* their motivation. Unless your customer wants something as soon as possible, they are not motivated. Often people come to me and ask me if I'll help them build a successful business. I ask them when they want to start. If they say, "Oh, sometime in the future," I always tell them to go away and come back when they are ready to start. Like ready to start *that day*! Unless someone wants something urgently, they will not be motivated, they will not do what it takes to become successful. If someone walks into a car salesroom and says they are looking for a new car, but then they say they are thinking about buying it next year, there is no point in trying to close a deal with them because they are not ready to buy; they might have a reason, but it's not urgent. It's very hard to close a deal with an unmotivated customer, but if you know their timeframe, then you know *when* they will become motivated. If they are not ready now, you need to use a different tactic. Take their details and follow up at regular intervals until they are ready to buy. This is a basic "call-back" strategy.

Point 2C: Find out what they can afford   You must know your customer's budget before you can sell them anything. If you go to buy a new car, the salesman will say, "What is your budget?" If you go to a wedding planner to plan your dream wedding, they will ask you, "What is your budget?" You can't plan anything without knowing how much you can or want to spend. So you can only sell something to someone if you know their budget. Having said that, remember that most people will downplay their real budget. They will say one figure but they will also have a contingency amount. If you start by showing them products (say cars) that are within their budget, and then they start asking to see some more expensive models, you know they have some contingency. But there is definitely no point in showing them products that are completely out of their price range.

Find out your customer's motivation. What is driving them?
Get their timeframe. You can't close a deal with an unmotivated customer.
You must know your customer's budget before you can sell them anything.

3: Close the Deal

This is obviously the most important part of the whole process. There is no transaction, no revenue for you, until you close the deal. So many business owners create great products that people need, form good relationships with their customers from effective marketing strategies, but still don't close the deal, because they simply don't know *how* to. You must learn to close, or you will not establish a successful business. There is a process to this, too. First you do a **test close**, then you **handle any objections**, and finally you actually go ahead and **ask for the deal**.

Point 3A: Test close   Before you go for the real close, it's useful to know where you are, on a scale of 1 to 10, in terms of your chances of closing the deal. A test close gives you an indication of where you stand, whereas a hard close has a definite answer. When you go for a hard close, you effectively ask, "Do you want this product, yes or no?" This is a closed question. Before you ask this, find out where you stand; work out how far the scales are tipped in your direction. A test close is a softer approach and can include questions such as "How are you feeling about this now?" and "What are your thoughts and do you have any questions?" or perhaps "Right now, based on what we've spoken about, how do you feel about the product? Let me get some feedback from you." Your customer's answers help you work out whether they are close to making a decision or whether they need more information from you.

Point 3B: Handle any objections   I could (and probably will one day) write an entire book on handling objections! It is a fascinating part of the psychology of selling. When people give you an objection, it is not usually because they don't want the product (you wouldn't be trying to sell it to them if they *really* didn't need it). Most objections are, in fact, your potential customers' way of saying, "I need more information." They are usually simply not confident about the information you have given them. On the other hand, some objections are false, they are just excuses that people give when they genuinely just don't want to buy the product. You need to be able to identify false objections (showing you that the customer is not interested and thus it would be a waste of your time to continue trying to sell to them) and objections that are a disguised request for more information. This is a skill that takes time to perfect and you can only really develop this skill through practice.

Point 3C: Ask for the deal   I'm always amazed to see how many people get right to the finish line, having worked really hard to get there, and yet simply don't take that final step across it. If you've done your job right and you've got to this point, dealing with any real objections along the way, then the answer to "Do you want to buy this product now?" should be an automatic yes. **But you do have to ask the question.** Don't be afraid. *You* know your customer needs it, and you've shown them that they need it; you know that they can *afford* it and that they are *motivated* to buy it now. There is no reason why the customer should say, "No" to the question. The reason most people find this question hard to ask is that they ask it before time. People make the mistake of trying to close before going through the deal-closing *process.* They try to negotiate *before* they find out if the person wants the product or not; that's the wrong way around. There are plenty of points throughout the process where you can figure out if the customer is going to say no (for example if they are not motivated, or they cannot afford it), in which case you should stop the process. If you have got all the way to the point of asking for the close, and you've gone through the correct process, the answer should automatically be YES! This whole process is your *qualification* process. You are qualifying buyers – finding out if they need and can afford your product, and if they are motivated (i.e. need it *now*). You should only continue to speak to **qualified potential buyers**.

Use a test close before going for a hard close to gauge customer's motivation. Handle any objections before going for the close. Finally … ASK FOR THE CLOSE! If you've done your job right, the answer will be YES!

The MPST Process for Successful Selling

Selling is a detailed process and it's important to get every element right. You really need to get experience and to keep getting more and more experience to develop good selling skills, but there are still many underlying factors that you can learn about the selling process. Some of what we have already gone through in this chapter can be applied in the "MPST" formula for selling. In the next chapter, we will be going through the sales machine, as well as traffic and conversion. MPST stands for: Motivated Buyers, Products, Sales Machine, and Traffic and Conversion.

1. **Motivated Buyers**

    As outlined above, when you have something to sell, you must find **motivated buyers**. If your customer does not want your product urgently, you are going to have a hard time selling to them. Finding and qualifying motivated buyers must be the first part of your selling process. The more motivated a potential customer is, the less work you have to do in order to convince them to buy.

2. **Products**

    As I have said many times, creating the right product is essential. You do this by choosing the right market, by finding out what your market needs, and by designing the right product. Then you test to find the delivery method of that product that will give you optimum sales. If you haven't designed a product that people want and need, you will struggle to sell it. It still amazes me how many times I see someone design a product that no one wants or needs.

3. **Sales Machine**

We will learn more about this in the next chapter. Your sales machine is the engine room of your business. Without a working sales machine you won't get the sales you need. When you perfect the efficiency of your sales machine, you will maximise your business potential. The other elements mentioned here – the products, motivated buyers, and traffic and conversion – are, in some ways, parts of the machine, but the machine itself is a system that needs to work optimally. In the next chapter we will look at how to build the best possible sales machine for your business.

4. **Traffic and Conversion**

You feed traffic into your sales machine, and you get conversions out. Whatever your business is, think of it as a shop. **Traffic** is the people walking past your shop, **leads** are people browsing in your shop, and **conversion** is when people buy something. That shop can be a physical one, or it can be online. Again, we will look at this in more detail in the next chapter.

3

Building Your Sales Machine

N ow that we've gone over how to choose, market and sell your products, let's look more closely at how you find the people who are going to become your customers.

As I described above, a big component of your sales plan has to be the process by which you find your motivated sellers, introduce them to your products and convert your leads into sales. How do you find your leads and how do you convert them into sales? You have great products, there may be many motivated customers out there just waiting for your products, and you may have great negotiating skills to convert your traffic into sales, but how does it all come together?

All these components are, in fact, the essential parts of your **sales machine**.

What is a machine? A machine is a system into which you put one thing and – assuming your machine is working – get a desired output. A good, simple analogy is to think of a coffee vending machine. You put a coin in and press the buttons for your desired coffee (number of shots, whether you want milk or sugar) and hopefully your desired coffee will be the output. If you programme an extra shot cappuccino with sugar and you get a black tea, then your machine is not working. You have to design and programme your machine so that it gives you what you want. If your input is correct and your output is what you want, then your machine is working. A working machine should always give you the result you desire. Imagine a ticket machine in a railway station. You select the ticket you want (destination, single or return, off-peak or peak), then put your payment card in, type in your PIN and out comes your ticket. If you selected a return to Edinburgh, that's what you expect to get. If you get a single to Cardiff, there is no doubt that the machine is broken!

> **A working machine will always give you the result you desire.**

A sales machine should be designed so that when you put in your leads, you eventually get sales. For example, if, every time you put an advert in the local newspaper you got 100 calls, and of those 100 calls, 10 of them turn into sales, then you have a working sales machine, because your machine is giving you sales (your desired result) every time you put something into it (pay for the advert).

If it's so simple, why doesn't everyone do it?

Often, people fail because they don't want to spend the money on advertising. But that advert is your "input". If you don't put something into your machine, you won't get any results out. If you don't spend money on an ad in the first place, you won't get the 100 calls and you won't make the 10 sales. In other words, your machine won't work. Going back to the coffee machine, it's like expecting coffee without putting in your coin. If you don't put the coin in, you won't get the coffee out.

> **You have to put something IN to get something OUT.**

It's amazing how many people understand this concept but don't act on it. Sometimes, people spend the money on the advertising but, because they don't get the results they want (for example, they only get 50 calls and two sales when they wanted 100 calls and 10 sales), they blame the *entire* machine, rather than investigating which part needs fixing. They stop using the machine altogether. Well that's one way of guaranteeing getting *no* results! And rarely is the entire machine broken. Going back to our coffee vending machine analogy, if you don't get the right coffee out, maybe there is a glitch in the programme, or it needs a new filter, or it's run out of sugar.

You don't need to throw out the whole machine or go without coffee just because it's run out of sugar! You call the company that services the machine and they come and fix it (replacing the sugar) and then you *pay them for it*, and then your coffee machine is working correctly again. You can't get your machine working without investing some money.

When your machine doesn't work, work on fixing it. *Invest* in fixing it.

Maybe your advertising strategy is not working, but you can't say advertising *per se* doesn't work. We see successful advertising campaigns around us all day, every day. We all respond to them, according to our tastes and buying strategies. We all know marketing and advertising works... we just have to find how it can work for our own businesses and products. We have to find the most efficient sales machine that gives us the best results. To do this, we have to test and measure the components of our machine constantly, in order to work out our most effective campaign. Only by testing and measuring can we find out what *doesn't* work, which brings us closer to what *does* work.

I constantly hear people complaining about the cost of advertising. When I hear those complaints, I point out that they have to stop seeing advertising as a *cost* and start to see it as an *investment*.

I also ask them to consider the cost of *not* advertising.

> **Don't think about the cost of advertising, think of the cost of not advertising. And advertising is not a cost; it's an investment.**

Advertising ROI (Return on Investment)

I once spent £1,500 on a Facebook ad campaign. I tracked my results closely and worked out that I made a £4,600 profit from the sales I made as a direct result of this campaign. In other words, the return on my investment was £3,100. That's over 200% return, a great return on my investment! That wasn't "expensive". Quite the reverse, that investment *made* me a lot of money. If I said to someone, "I spent £1,500 on a Facebook ad campaign," and they say, "Wow, that's expensive, I only paid £50," I'll ask them how much money they made from that £50. If they say nothing but "at least I didn't lose too much," guess what I say? "Well, your advert cost £3,150 more than mine so I'd say that's a pretty big loss!" That usually shuts them up pretty quickly!

Yes, I spent £1,500, but if I hadn't spent it, I wouldn't have made the profit.

Everyone with a business has to advertise. Even Richard Branson, with his successful Virgin brand, has to advertise constantly. And even he can't guarantee business success. In 2012, Branson launched his domestic airlines, "Little Red" to compete with British Airways on domestic flights within the UK. The business never quite took off and he had to stop "Little Red" operations in 2015 because of poor ticket sales. To me, that simply says that his sales machine wasn't working, and he couldn't figure out how to fix it. Because there is no obvious *reason* why a new domestic airline launched by Richard Branson shouldn't work (he had great success in the US and Australia with his domestic airlines in those countries). He knows how to run an airline, and there is plenty of business in the UK domestic market. So something was wrong with his sales machine. I would guess that he simply didn't get his advertising campaign right.

The biggest companies in the world still have to advertise; and increasingly they are taking their advertising campaigns online. Coca-Cola, McDonald's and KFC are some of the world's most recognisable brands, but they never stop bombarding people with advertisements. Just take a look at the banners on your emails and social media streams. You can hardly go a day without seeing an advert for one of these companies on your TV screens or computer screens.

I get frustrated when people come to me for help with their business and they don't want to spend any money. When they won't invest in advertising and promotion, I explain to them that *you can't get something out if you put nothing in!* Again, in the simplest terms this is like saying, "I want a coffee from this vending machine but I'm not prepared to put my money in." If you take this attitude, you will wait forever for your coffee! You can't have a "million-dollar" *dream* with a "minimum-wage" *work ethic,* just like you can't have a million-dollar lifestyle with a 10-dollar mindset. The reason many businesses are broke is because they don't invest enough in the right places.

Some people seem to resent spending money on anything. It's not just their business that they won't spend money on … I've seen plenty of people who don't want to spend money on themselves, either. They won't buy new clothes or a decent car; they won't even spend money on their health. Whatever you spend – on your business or on yourself – is an *investment.* If you put nothing in, you'll get nothing out. The *more* you put in, the *more* you will get out.

Imagine two entrepreneurs turning up to a meeting with potential investors. They have equally good business plans and ideas. The investors only want to invest in one business. One of the entrepreneurs is wearing an old suit that has a stain on it and has a few holes in it, because he's decided not to spend money on a new suit (seeing it as an unnecessary expense). The other entrepreneur is wearing a new suit. If the business plans are equally good, the entrepreneurs equally impressive in their managerial abilities, and there is no other deciding factor, who do you think will get the investment? And how much will that decision not to buy a new suit have ultimately cost the first entrepreneur?

Many people simply don't understand that they don't need to put every penny they have into advertising, they just need to find the *right* amount to put in. They are literally *afraid* of advertising; they perceive it as a risk that could cripple their business if they don't get the required results. But advertising is a necessary part of any business plan, and is as important as the manufacture of the goods and services you are creating. You have to budget for advertising as one of your operating costs. You wouldn't spend *all* your money on product development, but you have to spend *some* on product development or you will have nothing to sell. It's exactly the same with advertising ... you don't spend everything on it, but you have to spend something or you will not have a fully functioning sales machine. Even if you do not get the results you want from a particular advertising campaign, your investment was not wasted because you learned something valuable. You learned what *didn't* work.

As the great British inventor Sir James Dyson says, "Enjoy failure and learn from it. You can never learn from success."

> Enjoy failure and learn from it. You can never learn from success.
>
> —James Dyson

The Learning Process

I love the learning process. I will always invest in my education. Every day I learn something new. I still get things wrong and have to start again with the lessons I've learned. And I still challenge myself. For example, I've always had a burning desire to learn the guitar but I just never seemed to get around to it. A while ago I decided I simply had to "go for it". I bought a guitar and started playing. At first, obviously, I sounded terrible. But I kept practising. I practised the same four chords over and over again. I also tried to sing at the same time as playing, which made the guitar bit even harder to focus on. At one point my fingers were almost raw but finally, after about six months or so, I was able to play something recognisable as a song. Okay I'm never going to be Jimi Hendrix or Ed Sheeran, but I was proud of my achievement! With patience and practice I believe you can learn to do almost anything.

Most of the things I'm good at now, I've had to practise hard to perfect. Often, when I come off stage after speaking to a big audience, I get people coming up to me saying, "Wow, you're a natural born speaker," but nothing could be further from the truth! You should see some of the videos of me speaking when I was first starting out; they are terrible! I'm a big believer in what Malcolm Gladwell says in his book *Outliers*. He believes that it takes 10,000 hours to become an expert in something. It's all about investing the time, and applying yourself to the practice.

I'm pretty sure I'm close to having spent 10,000 hours on stage public speaking, so I feel justified in calling myself an expert. I worked it out by figuring out that, at a weekend event I can spend three days speaking on stage for eight hours each day. That's 24 hours in total. If I speak at an average of 30 events per year that's 720 hours, and I've been doing this (to date) for around 12 years, so that's approximately 8,640 hours I've spent speaking on stage. So I'm getting up there … getting close to that 10,000 hours it takes to become an expert by Malcolm Gladwell's standards!

With practice comes confidence. It used to take me days, maybe weeks to prepare for an event. These days I can jump on stage any time, anywhere, with very little notice and deliver a decent programme. I've done it so many times it's ingrained in my head.

When you are well practised, everything speeds up. If you came to me now and said, "John, I urgently need new leads for my business,"

I could generate a whole list of new leads in just two hours. Why? Because I've been doing it so long I know all the short cuts. What would take someone else weeks or even months would take me a matter of hours. I can generate leads and make profit very easily, but that's my reward for educating myself… for learning how to do it. If you don't *educate* yourself, if you don't *learn*, then you don't get any of the rewards.

Now let's go through the various components of the sales machine.

Funnels

Your sales machine starts with your funnels. An effective sales strategy must include a way of **funnelling** people into your sales machine. These people are like the "coins" that you need to put into the machine in order to get your results (sales) out. In the second part of this book we will look at the latest ways of reaching people in the ever-evolving digital age – including using social media platforms – but in this section we are going to look at the ways in which we have been funnelling people into our sales machines in the digital era so far.

When creating funnels we are always looking at new ways to capture data, to ensure we get contact details from people in order to funnel them into our sales machine. If they are endlessly "sold to", people get jaded, so we have to look at innovative ways of persuading them to sign up to receive information from us.

Your funnel is basically the **bridge** that channels your traffic into your website; it literally *funnels* people to your sales page. Your marketing strategy is a fundamental part of your funnel. Your marketing efforts are designed to *educate* people on why they need to buy your product. One of the most important functions of your funnel is to take your traffic on a *journey* so that they end up at your sales page as **educated visitors**.

You can't allow any of your valuable traffic to skip parts of the journey. If I post an ad offering a certain course and people click through that ad to arrive at my website without taking a journey, and there they suddenly learn that the course is going to cost them £1,000, they might say that it costs too much and click off the site. They were obviously interested in the first place, but I have lost them because I haven't **educated** them, slowly, showing them *why* the course is worth £1,000. If they have been taken through a *funnel* that educates them as to why the course costs £1,000, and tells them exactly what the value of that particular course is to them, they will be more likely to buy the course.

The Product Staircase Funnel

During the journey, you can still sell lower-priced products to people as part of their education. That way, you are making sales while you are educating them. Sales funnels help build loyal customers. In sales, **commitment** and **consistency** are vital. If you want someone to commit to spending £1,000 on a product, you are more likely to get that sale if you start by getting them to commit to spending just £10 for a related product. Then you get them to pay £100 for a slightly more advanced and valuable product. At the next stage, you charge them £500 for an even more sophisticated product, and eventually, if your products are high quality and give your customers the value they were expecting, not only will they be more likely to pay the £1,000 for your main product, but you will have made more money along the funnel (£1,610 in this example) than if they'd gone straight to the £1,000 product. I call this the **product staircase funnel**.

I have seen this process work time and time again. I know that if 1,000 people download a free video I've offered, 100 people will buy the £50 e-book that is offered at the end of the video, and 10 people will buy the £500 course that follows on from the information given in the e-book.

Every funnel has steps and stages. I also use the **seminar funnel**. My experience has shown me that if 1,000 people register for a free event, about 150 people will attend it and some 50 people will buy the product I am selling at the event.

At the most basic level, any funnel is a **conversion funnel**. I always encourage my property business students to think in terms of conversion funnels. If you get 100 enquiries from people who want to sell their property, around 10 will say yes to making a deal with you, and of those 10 (after some drop out, or you find problems with the property, etc.) you will probably have one that will go through to complete a sale. Figure 3.1 shows you your formula: that you need 100 enquiries for every one sale.

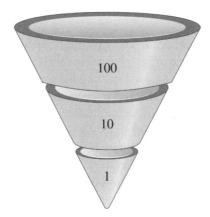

Figure 3.1   The Conversion Funnel

As its very shape would suggest, a funnel is basically a numbers game. So the important element is feeding as many people into that funnel as possible – in other words, driving as much traffic to your initial site as possible.

Conversion Strategies

Why are we talking about conversion strategies before we talk about generating traffic? Because you must ensure your conversion strategy works, that you have good conversion rates before you drive potential customers to your site, otherwise you will lose all those potential customers that you've worked hard to put into your funnel.

All the factors outlined below contribute to whether or not people will buy your product when they arrive at your site, therefore **you must get these elements right** *before* **you start generating traffic**. This is critical. Most people worry about traffic and then conversion, but **it's the other way around!** What's the point of sending a million people to your website if you haven't checked that you can convert this amazing volume of traffic into sales. It would be a complete waste. *First* you work on giving yourself the best possible chance of getting a high conversion rate, and *then* you spend the money on driving as many people as possible to your site.

Ensure your conversion strategies work before driving traffic to your site!

Why Conversion Comes First

Most people find out the hard way that *optimising your conversion rate comes before generating traffic*. That's certainly my experience. Later, I will tell a story about the time I spent a fortune on online advertising before I had tested and perfected my conversion rates. My money was wasted because all those potential customers who were driven to my website thanks to my great advertising simply clicked off it because, at the time, the quality of the site was not good enough and the messaging did not keep them interested. So much of what drives me is the desire to help other people avoid making the costly (in terms of both money and time) mistakes that I made!

Earlier we identified the basic steps of taking a product to market as:

1. Choose a sizeable market.
2. Find out what your market wants and needs.
3. Design the product or service that your market needs.
4. Sell that product to your market.

Now I want to break down "sell that product to your market" further. This one is actually made up of a few more steps, which include attracting a huge amount of traffic, converting that traffic, and then capturing and storing customers' details for repeat business. So let's look at it again and consider the steps to be:

1. Choose a sizeable market.
2. Know what your market wants and needs.
3. Design the product or service that your market needs.
4. **Attract a huge amount of traffic.**
5. **Convert as much traffic as possible (sell your product).**
6. **Keep customers' details on a database to sell further products to them.**

You *have* to get every step right or you won't sell products. And once the process is working, once your sales machine has been perfected, then it works in that order, but *before* you set the wheels in motion, you have to work Steps 4, 5 and 6 backwards to ensure you are ticking all the boxes. In other words, *before* you start creating your "huge amount of traffic", you must make sure you have the means to keep customers' details on a database and ensure you are getting the best conversion rates.

Improving your Conversion Rate

What is a good conversion rate? Ideally, of course, we want a conversion rate of 100%, but we know that we'll never even get close to that. Our funnel will narrow as people drop out. However, there are several elements that help keep people on track and in the sales funnel. If you get these elements right in the first place, you are on your way to a improving your conversion rate.

The areas to focus on if you want to improve your conversion rate are:

1. **Relevance of Messaging**

   You have to ensure you keep your messaging on your links relevant. This sounds obvious but I've seen people make some critical mistakes. If I want to buy a calculator and I see an advertisement for calculators but the link takes me to a page where I can buy a phone, I'm more than likely going to click off that page. It sounds illogical that someone would post an advertisement for a calculator in order to sell phones, but I've seen people do the most absurd things thinking that they will "trick" people into looking at their products. No one wants to be *tricked* into anything! Your advertisement *must* be relevant to what you are selling. The "advertising calculators to sell phones" example is obviously quite an extreme one, but I use it to show people how it can hurt your sales if you don't get your messaging right. If you're advertising baby clothes because you think that will get people to click onto your site where you want to sell them adult clothes, your messaging is wrong.

2. **Content and Copy**

   Everything that is written on your page helps to sell your product. If you have copy or content that is badly written or carries misinformation it will *hurt* your conversion rates. Your sales copy is vital. Your descriptions must be accurate and easy to understand. You must also have exactly the right amount of content: too little and people will feel uninformed; too much and people will feel overwhelmed with information. The copy should make the product look attractive and inviting; it should tell the customer exactly why they need this product and what it will do for them. Remember to **sell the benefits**. Your content and copy must speak to what your potential customers *want*. Also think about your choice of words. Words are incredibly powerful. The words you choose will evoke different feelings in people. Words have different strengths. For example, the word "shark" is much punchier than the word, "dolphin" because of the associations with each animal. You can describe things in so many different ways and each way has a different weight. For example, "passed away" has a different weight to the word "died", it doesn't feel quite as heavy. In most cases, you *want* copy that is going to be "heavy" or make a greater impact. When you are writing copy, imagine weighing scales. The more weight you stack on, the more powerful your website becomes. The "heavier" your message gets, the more likely people are to buy. You need to use weighty words to tip the scales towards people taking action. The words you use are *so* important. For example if you ask in an email, "Do you want to alter your life?" a few people might respond. If you ask, "Do you want to change your life?" a few more might come on board. But if you ask, "Do you want to *transform* your life?" you'd probably get the biggest response. Out of the words "alter, change and transform", "transform" carries the most weight. Imagine posting an ad that read, "Click here if you think you might like to alter your life sometime in the future." Far fewer people would take action than if you wrote, "**Click here if you want to TRANSFORM your life NOW**." We are selling the benefits *and* the urgency with this statement. Once you have written the best copy, you will use it everywhere – in your emails, your ads and on your website. You must sell the *why*. The "why" really has to "burn"; people will not take action when they are comfortable. You have to make them uncomfortable and fully aware of the negative consequences of *not* having this product. Instead of saying, "If you don't adopt a healthier diet you will get fat," you have to say, "If you don't adopt a healthier diet you could DIE!"

3. **Price**

Is your product reasonably priced for what it is? How does it compare in price to other similar products that are available online? Price is a fluctuating element. You must keep doing your research to check that you are at the best price point. You can keep adjusting your price as you test your conversion rate, to ensure that you are priced at the optimal point. **Make sure your price doesn't hurt your conversion rates.**

4. **Product**

Over and above all else, the quality and relevance of your product is still your first priority. You must ensure your product is something people want and need. I see so many people put a tremendous amount of time and money into their marketing, which all goes to waste if they don't have a product people actually want and need. It may be that *they* don't know they want and need it yet, but as long as you've done your research and *you* know that they want and need it, you've got it right. But you *must* do that research and testing first. Remember, no amount of marketing and sales techniques will sell people a product that they don't want or need.

5. **Offer**

Obviously you are ultimately offering your product or service for sale, but there are all kinds of enticements you can offer customers in order to encourage them to buy. How can you make the purchase sound more attractive and enticing? How can you position your offer to make people think they are getting a great deal? You could say, "Buy one today and get the next one free." Or you could put a time limit on your offer, such as, "Buy today at this price as the price goes up tomorrow." Think of all the ways in which you can encourage people to buy when they might be wavering. Look at how your competitors are doing it. You don't want someone making an offer that you can't match.

6. **Trust**

What can you do to gain people's trust? Well, you can start by being completely transparent. **Transparency** is key. You must include a phone number and address on your website so that your customers know that they have a way to reach you if they need to. **Credibility** is also important. Ensure you publicise any recognisable name of someone who is happy to endorse you. If I visit a website that has several logos of recognisable companies on it, I am assured of the credibility of that site. You really should have some endorsements to build trust in your potential customers.

Converting in Person

Converting an interested prospective customer into a sale can happen in many ways and happens at different stages of the sales process. Converting online traffic into online sales is great. But often, especially for more expensive products, you need to get in front of those potential customers to close the sale. My strategy and process depends on whether I am giving a webinar or a live preview event for a course.

1. **The Webinar**

   A webinar is, literally, a seminar that is given online. I give a presentation that people can view online, either live or at a later time. When I give a seminar, I'm hoping to convert several people by getting them to click through to my website to buy a product. Over the years, I've perfected the structure of my presentations and have a formula that I have found maximises the conversions I make.

   In order, I cover the following:

   Social proof: I will tell a case study to show how I helped someone else achieve whatever it is I'm offering to help my audience do.

   My story: I tell my own personal journey. I don't focus on how successful I am today, I tell them all about my humble beginnings and how I worked my way to the top. Remember, every story needs a beginning, middle and end. You must explain exactly where you started, describe your struggle through the bad times, and then conclude with the ending, explaining exactly how and when you finally succeeded.

   Create need: I always explain exactly why they *need* what I'm offering.

   Sell the problems: I explain the consequences of *not* having this product. If you were selling a diet programme, you'd go on about what will happen if the potential customer keeps eating junk food, how it would lead to serious health problems.

Sell the solution: after explaining why they *need* my product and the *problems* they will encounter without it, I **sell the solution**. I tell them what the product is and what it does. I explain exactly *how* and *why* it will be the solution to my customers' existing and potential problems.

Make a clear CALL TO ACTION: I make sure I explain to people what they need to do immediately in order to take up the opportunity. I give them a link to one of my websites where they can sign up, or I give them a number to call (making sure there will be someone at the end of the line, or a way for them to leave their details.) You could also use this opportunity to give away a free sample of the product you are offering, which will encourage them to take up the call to action.

You could, of course, apply all of the above to any face-to-face situation where you have the opportunity to make a sale.

2. **The Live Preview Event**

    I approach my live preview events a little differently from a webinar because I am hoping to convert people *in the room* as opposed to sending them off to a website or giving them a phone number to call. In this instance I have my potential customers *in front of me in person*, so it's a great opportunity.

    A preview event is where I will invite people to a specified location and give a live presentation. Within the presentation, I am giving them education, but I am also hoping to inspire them to buy a product. Getting people to buy something is a process. People only buy from people they like and trust, and the process of getting people to like and trust you can take some time.

    The specific steps I follow during a live event are as follows:

    Introduce and engage: as soon as I've introduced myself I ensure that I engage with the audience and thank them for coming. I always acknowledge the efforts they've made to get there: the fact that they've travelled there (I invite people to call out a few places they have travelled from) and have possibly taken time off work or maybe organised childcare.

I acknowledge the fact that they are investing their time and money in something that is going to help them.

Ensure participation: next I ask the audience two questions that ensure I get 100% participation. The two questions are slightly different but both should get positive responses and between them should cover why most people are there. Imagine your product is a weight-loss programme. First you could ask: "Raise your hand if you would like to lose weight in the next four weeks," and then, "Raise your hand if you would like to lose weight healthily." If someone didn't raise their hand to either of those questions, there's not much point in them being there! And these questions help to wake people up and get them focused. Most people are still half-asleep when arrive, and they will stay that way unless you wake them up; it's your *job* to wake them up, it is imperative that you do wake them up and make them listen to you. You must engage with them right the way through the presentation; if you stop, it's hard to win them back.

Get their attention (WIIFT): I always, always let the audience know WIIFT (**what's in it for them**). As I mentioned above … sell the problems. Make your questions very detailed; discuss their problems. Show them you understand their pain. Using the weight loss example, you could say, "I know you are all here because your have been trying to lose weight. You've tried so many diets and when you lose it, it never stays off." Once you've shown them you understand their "problem", next you tell them WIIFT. You can say, "But today we are going to show you how you can lose weight effectively and healthily so that you will never put it back on again." You are going to help them solve their problems. You are identifying their problem and showing them how you are going to help them solve it.

At the end of the day, all people really want to know is *what's in it for them*. I've tested many different formats, and this is the one place where you can easily go wrong; if you don't tell them what's in it for them at this early stage, they will lose interest and you won't get them back. You must cover this as soon as you have introduced yourself, engaged with them and got them to participate by answering a couple of questions.

By telling them WIIFT, you get their attention. After this, you should have hooked their attention because they know you are going to add value to their lives.

Tell them *why* they should listen to you. This is the point at which you present your credibility, your authority. You need to put some of your own story in here because at this point they are all thinking the same thing: "Why should I listen to you? Who are you?" So here is where you tell your "story of struggle". You can make it into a "before and after" story, but make sure you tell the whole story (although keep it short and to the point). The mistake most speakers make when they get up on stage is that they talk about themselves for too long. Once you have shown that you've got a valid story and you know what you're talking about because you've shown them what you've achieved, get back to WIIFT.

Give them content. I'm amazed by how many times I've seen people stand up to talk to a room full of potential customers and give them *no content*. They fill the time talking about themselves, and asking questions to engage the audience, but ultimately give no content. You must give content early on. You must give them what they've come for. This is your opportunity to show them what you can teach them. Don't hold back here. You have a short window in which to grab them with what you can teach them. Make it dramatic. And keep the attention on you; so ***don't use slides***. I use a flipchart but I don't use slides. If you use slides everyone puts their attention on the slides. You need their attention on you. You want them to be looking at you at all times so that you can *engage* with them. In my experience I find that **slides kill engagement**. You must keep your audience's attention; they will learn more by listening to you. Also, when you show slides, you give away the punchline; people can see it before you say it. This is why I only use a flip chart, so that I can show it *as* I explain it. I keep everyone in the moment, keeping it live and immediate. I tell them what I'm going to I tell them, which creates anticipation, which in turn creates interest and attention. If I walk over to the flip chart and I say, "I'm going to tell you *one* thing and it's going to change your life," I create great anticipation and ensure engagement.

The transition. When you make the transition from the free content you have given to the product you are offering for sale, it has to be a gradual shift. You can't be too blunt otherwise it will jar with your audience. It's like when a DJ is mixing records together; if he just stops one and immediately starts the other, it will sound uncomfortable. A good DJ will mix two records together for a few seconds to make the transition smooth, so the mixing of the records is seamless. You must make a smooth transition because the moment you start selling to them, people put their guards up. If you make a smooth, seamless transition they will go along with you, and be more likely to buy.

The irresistible offer. Give your audience a "no brainer" offer; ensure it makes so much sense that it would be crazy *not* to get it now. By the time you are making your offer, people should be thinking, "I definitely need this so I may as well get it here and now because I'll regret it if I don't." An offer should be designed so that it virtually sells itself. Using the weight loss programme example again, your offer should be as *irresistible* as if you are saying, "Take this pill and you will instantly lose weight." The offer has to show that it will give people **the result they want**. At this point, also make sure you have justified your price so that no one has the excuse of objecting over price.

The special offer and call to action. You can increase conversion rates by making your audience a special one-time offer and including an immediate call to action. You could say, "If you get this product today, I'll give you a second one free. If you sign up before the next session, you will also get a further 20% off." Make it a one-time offer and time-sensitive.

Generating Traffic

Once you have optimised every other part of your sales machine, and *only* when you have optimised every part of your sales machine, you ready to start generating traffic. So before you start driving as much traffic as you can to your site, you must check that:

1. You have chosen a sizeable market.
2. You have tested what your market wants and needs.

3. You have designed a product that your market wants and needs.

4. You know your conversion strategies *work*!

If any of the above steps are not right yet, **get them right before driving traffic to your sales page or you will be wasting your money**! How do you get traffic? You get traffic from marketing and advertising. I've already stressed the importance of investing in advertising, but how did advertising, and the platforms for advertising, evolve?

Advertising as a concept has been around for hundreds of years, but it really came into its own with the surge of capitalism. Back in the nineteenth century, advertising platforms were limited to print, in newspapers and posters. Then came commercial radio and television. Advertising soon became a flourishing industry as companies increased their budgets to enable them to record and broadcast ever more sophisticated adverts. The dawning of the Internet age massively reduced advertising costs and brought down barriers to entry. The introduction of Google AdWords allowed anyone to advertise electronically on relevant websites. Recently, social media platforms (such as Facebook, Instagram, Twitter, LinkedIn and more) have become popular advertising platforms. We will look at some of these more closely in Part II.

As well as paid advertising, you can also use direct marketing to generate traffic. This involves doing things like sending out physical leaflets to names and addresses on mailing lists, or sending out emails to a list of email addresses. You create mailing lists by keeping contact details of all the people who have bought or shown interest in your products. You can also buy mailing lists from other people. And you can reach potential customers through referrals, partnerships and sponsorship deals. Obviously, you must ensure you abide by data protection regulations in the country you are operating in.

You have to work out your marketing and advertising strategy before you invest money in it. I've seen people sink £10k into a radio advert hoping they might capture the attention of potential customers without doing any planning around the best time and place to air that ad. If you don't *plan* wisely, you could be throwing away your money. What if your advert plays at a time when your ideal demographic is not listening? Or on a radio station that your demographic doesn't listen to? Then all your money would have been wasted. That's an expensive way of finding out what doesn't work!

You can always find information that will tell you when your ideal demographic is listening, and which stations they listen to, even if you have to pay for specific information. This will enable you to do the most accurately **targeted marketing**.

Exposure and Engagement

In every marketing and advertising campaign you must look at how much **exposure** and **engagement** you can get. The key goal is to get as much exposure and engagement as possible.

Securing Exposure

There's an old saying that goes, "In business, it is not who you know but who knows *you*." You need exposure.

There are two basic types of exposure: **free** and **paid**. You could also call these **slow** (free) and **fast** (paid). In other words, free exposure is slow, paid exposure is fast. Even on social media, since the surge of advertising on social media platforms, you get slow (free) and fast (paid) advertising. Facebook offers slow (building your pages for free and inviting people to like them) and fast (paid ads designed to drive more traffic to your page) exposure. If you're serious about building your business you preferably want fast exposure. If you don't want to pay for it, read what I wrote above again, about advertising being an *investment* not a cost – and a crucial investment!

Let's look at how this works on Google.

You can get free exposure on Google by ensuring that your website comes up first on searches. But this is a slow and laborious process and you have to do a huge amount of search engine optimisation (SEO) work to get your site to rank higher than anyone else's. Say, for example, you are an accountant in Croydon. Of course you want to ensure that your site comes up first when someone Googles "Croydon accountant". But so does your competition. You would have to work very hard at making sure your site gets to the top of the Google search engine, and it will take an extremely long time. It can take three to six months just to get Google to index your site in the first place!

If you want to get exposure faster, you have to pay to come up in searches; for this you use a Google Ad. Google AdWords allows you to place an advert in the search results so that when people search for the word that you've selected, your advert comes up. For example, if you're selling fitness training in Newcastle, and you choose the AdWord "fitness specialist Newcastle", then every time a person types that into the Google search engine, your ad will be shown.

You can also use Google to purchase advertising space on other people's websites, which is just like purchasing space on a billboard or in a newspaper. But you *must* learn how to use Google's AdWords correctly and efficiently or you could very quickly lose your entire advertising budget with no results … as I learned to my cost!

Now, as I promised earlier, it's time to tell you about one of my most costly mistakes!

Google AdWords: A Cautionary Tale

Google is a fantastic resource and has many invaluable tools. It is also the most used search engine in the world with over 90% share of the market (as of October 2018), so we can't really operate and do business without engaging with Google. But be warned; Google loves to spend your money! In my early days of online marketing, I fell victim to the Google money-making machine.

When I was looking for ways to market and advertise my products, I came across Google AdWords. I went online and searched for help with using Google AdWords. I found some free instructional videos on YouTube and watched them. They basically told me to follow all Google's instructions. Looking back, I should have been more cautious, because it wasn't as if these videos were telling me anything more than I could have gathered from reading Google's instructions. But I went ahead without researching further.

These random instructional videos I watched told me that, if I followed them my ads would appear on the first page of Google Search. I did everything, step by step. At some point along the way, there was a box that said, "Let Google choose how best to spend your advertising budget". This box wasn't mentioned on the instructional videos that I watched but it seemed pretty straightforward, so I ticked the box. Then I uploaded my ad and my bank account details, and waited for all the business to roll in.

A week later I was frustrated that I wasn't getting the sales I was expecting. I thought I might as well check my bank balance to find out how much money Google had spent. I discovered that Google had spent £12,000! In just *one week*!

I was obviously at fault because I should have been checking what Google was spending every day, maybe every hour, but I was still stunned to discover how much they had spent. Of course I'd blindly "agreed" to the terms and conditions without reading them (as most of us do) and technically Google had done nothing wrong, so there was no way I could get a refund. This was one of my harshest business lessons.

Since that time I have been more wary of the videos I find on YouTube. Remember, anyone can post a video to YouTube. If you are looking for reliable information you *must* do some research on the credibility of the person presenting or promoting it. This is an on-going issue on the Internet; having no barriers to entry creates a double-edged sword. No one is directly policing the quality of the content that is uploaded onto YouTube, so it is unsolicited and unreliable. You have to do your own due diligence to ensure the education you are getting has value.

But it wasn't just Google at fault here. Another part of my learning curve was that I didn't test whether all the components of my sales funnel were converting *before* all the money was spent. That wasn't Google's fault; that was my fault. As I explained earlier, at this stage I hadn't perfected and tested my website. No matter how much of my money Google spent, it was my fault that more traffic wasn't converting. I spent a fortune on an advertising campaign when I had a terrible website, so any traffic that arrived at my website would click straight off again.

Now, thankfully (and through trial and error) I have become an expert at using Google AdWords. I even teach a course on using Google AdWords. And yet I still get people who enquire about my course, decide not to spend the money on it (saying they are going to figure it all out for themselves) and then come back to me one month later to enrol on my course … after having lost twice the cost of the course on Google AdWords campaigns that didn't convert! It always pays dividends to learn from an expert. You've always got two choices. Either you spend your money on making mistakes and finding out how not to do something, or you can pay an expert to teach you. The problem is, if you spend the money on making the mistakes, you will probably discover you want to learn from the expert anyway, so you will have paid twice: once to get it wrong and once to learn how to do it right. It makes more sense to pay once, to learn from the expert in the first place.

Google AdWords is just a business tool. If you want to grow your business, you have to learn how to operate all the tools. You wouldn't drive a car without lessons, even if someone gave you operating instructions. Why do you think you can operate business tools without lessons? As I explain to people who are deliberating whether to hire me to help them: I've become an expert through my own trial and error; it will cost you much less to learn from my mistakes than to make your own. I know how to maximise your return. If you spend £1,000 on Google AdWords, you might get 10 leads. If *I* spend that £1,000, with the knowledge I have, I will probably get around 100 leads.

I always come across people who focus on *saving* money in their business. I explain to them that they should be looking at ways to *spend* their money, and increasingly *smarter* ways of spending it. You have to invest your money in your business and **let your money work for you**. When your money is in the bank, it is not working for you. You have to adopt this very powerful **sales mindset** if you want to be a successful business owner.

Remember… you don't *spend* money on advertising, you *invest* it; you don't *spend* money on educating yourself, you *invest* it.

> **You don't *spend* money on advertising … you *invest* it.**
> **You don't *spend* money on educating yourself … you *invest* it.**

PR: Free and Paid-for

Another way of gaining exposure is through PR. Again you can do *free* or *paid-for* PR.

Free PR: you can write articles about yourself for free and submit them to newspapers and magazines, but it might take a long time before you get anything published.

Paid PR: you can pay for an advertorial piece in a newspaper. A colour half-page in the nationwide edition of the free newspaper *The Metro* costs around £20,000 (at time of writing). Other newspapers differ in price. You can also hire a PR person. But make sure you are getting your money's worth. Ensure that the PR person has the right connections to get you the right interviews and exposure or you will be wasting your money. As ever, always do your research before spending your money.

PR is more about promotion than direct advertising or marketing. When people ask me to explain the difference between advertising and promotion I explain it like this:

Advertising copy would read: "Hi, I've got a delicious apple here that I'm selling for £1."

Promotional (PR) copy would read: "Oh wow, I've just tasted the best apple I've ever tasted in my life. You'd love this apple; you really must try it. I even have some I can sell to you for £1 per apple."

Engaging your Potential Customers

To engage people fully, first you must find out what they want. What can you give them *right now* that can help them? The more you know about your clients' needs, the more you can engage them, because you will know how to add value to their lives. You need to educate them and show them how you are the person who will bring the most value to their lives.

You should always be thinking about engagement. I am engaging with *you* right now! As the author of this book, I am engaging with you as the reader. I know what you want – help to improve your business – so I am keeping you engaged by talking about all the ways in which you can improve your business. Some of you may even end up coming to me as clients because I am showing you, *right now*, that I can add value to your business. I wrote this book to share my knowledge with you. I have more knowledge to share. I want to keep you engaged and tell you what I know. Furthermore, I'm showing you that writing a book, *per se*, is a fantastic way to get exposure and engage with people at the same time! If you want to write a book to help you position yourself as an expert in your market, I can also show you how to do that.

Getting Qualified Traffic

The final step in generating traffic is to ensure that your traffic is **qualified**. You need to ensure that the *right* people are being driven to your sales page; people who need what you are selling and people who are motivated to buy. This is where expert knowledge of Google AdWords can help. Your ads on Google help to qualify your traffic.

Again, qualifying traffic is an intricate process and takes practice.

To give you a brief example, when I wanted to drive people who were motivated to sell their houses to my website, I first used the phrase "SELL HOUSE" as my AdWords phrase. This meant that my ad would be shown to people who typed these exact words into their search engine. But I soon realised that this was too general and I was competing with countless estate agents and property investors. So next I tried "SELL HOUSE TODAY" and I found that this gave me people who were more motivated to sell their properties. Then I found that "SELL HOUSE FAST" worked even better. In the end, I discovered that "STOP REPOSSESSION" gave me the most motivated sellers.

Make sure you are using the best AdWords to get the most qualified traffic being driven to your website. This will always increase your conversion rates.

Test and Measure

You *must* **test and measure** in order to get your best results. I once paid a source £2,000 for four leads. Each lead cost me around £500 and not one of them bought a product. That was a direct loss of £2,000, a 0% return on my investment. I didn't consider the money completely wasted because I learned not to use that source again! Some time after this, I paid £900 to a different source. I got 240 leads (so that was £3.75 per lead) and two people bought £1,000 products. I took £2,000 from those leads, so I made a profit of £1,100, an ROI of over 100%! This showed me that the latter source gave me **qualified traffic**.

You can't predict; you can only test. Sometimes you will lose, sometimes you will break even, and sometimes you will make a profit. You need to know your break-even point, the point at which the cost of a lead is not profitable. And you need to know the maximum you can afford to pay per lead. In the example I gave above, my conversion rate was approximately one in 100 (I got two sales out of 240 leads). My product sold for £1,000. This tells me the maximum I can spend per lead from this source, on this particular campaign, is £10. At this point I would break even (so ideally I want to pay less than £10). If I paid any more than that, I would be running at a loss.

The average Internet conversion rate from online campaigns is a rather conservative 1%. If your conversion rate is less than one in 100, you have problems that you need to fix. Perhaps you are not qualifying your traffic; perhaps you are getting leads from the wrong socioeconomic group. Look at every cog in the machine to try to fix the problem.

How do you know what your conversion rate is? Well, like anything in life and business, you have to measure it. You test a campaign by sending some traffic to your site (through a small ad campaign) and seeing how many clicks you get and how many conversions you get. You then change one of the variables and test it again, seeing which one works better, i.e. gives you more conversions. You never test something in isolation; you must always test variables against each other (see the red/blue dress example given below). When you've found the variable that gives you your best conversion rate, you scale up the campaign.

You *must* measure your traffic and conversion rate. I am always stunned to discover how many people don't know their site statistics. You have to plan and budget for this. I've seen people spend all their money on designing a great-looking site, but they haven't made any plans to spend money on advertising, or on testing their marketing and conversion strategies.

Testing and measuring all the elements of your sales machine is an essential part of your sales process. You must invest in it. And it is an ongoing process; you have to keep testing because all markets fluctuate.

Remember, you don't spend on advertising, you *invest* in it; similarly you don't spend on testing and measuring, you *invest* in it.

We all want to improve our sales, but you can't improve something you can't measure. If you come to me and say you want to improve your time for a 5 K run, I'm going to ask you what time you are currently running 5 K in. If you say you don't know, I can't help you. How would you improve your time if you don't *know* your time? How are you ever going to improve your conversion rates if you don't *know* your conversion rates? If I don't know, every day, how many leads I'm getting, there is no way I can improve on those numbers.

Once your conversion rates are optimised, if you want more sales, you need to generate more traffic. But you still need to know how much traffic you are generating before you can improve on that number. When people say to me, "I want more traffic coming to my site," I ask them what their current figures are. If they don't know, I tell them they must find out before we can work on increasing their traffic.

What everyone actually wants, of course, is more *sales*. Increased sales come from increased traffic, and specifically increased *qualified* traffic. Once you have ensured that your sources are giving you **qualified traffic** and you have **optimised your conversion rate**, you are ready to increase your traffic. You have to work backwards and improve your number of hits (your traffic) before your sales figures will improve. It's all about reverse engineering.

Reverse Engineering

Reverse engineering means deciding the result you want and then working backwards to figure out what you need to put into place in the first instance in order to get to that place. In other words, what do you need to **feed into your machine** in order to get the results you want? You set your end goal then work backwards to figure out what you need to do to get there. You want a way of getting coffee at any time without having to go to a café … so you build a machine that produces coffee automatically when triggered by receiving coins that equal a certain amount.

Let's say you want to turn over a million pounds in sales this year. One way of turning over a million pounds is to sell 1,000 units of a product that costs £1,000. If I want to sell 1,000 units in one year, I need to ask myself: How many units do I need to sell per week? The answer to that is: approximately 19. So how many do I need to sell each day? That would be around three. Great! Now I know that, if I want to turn over a million pounds in sales this year, my target is to sell three units per day. Next I need to figure out how many leads I need in order to sell three units per day. If I have tested a campaign that has a conversion rate of three in 100 then I need 300 leads a day in order to sell three units a day.

To summarise, using reverse engineering I have worked out: **if I want to turn over £1 million per year, I need to get at least 300 qualified leads per day**. Now I need to find the most profitable way (least cost per qualified lead) of getting 300 qualified leads per day.

Know your Stats!

You cannot hope to have an optimised, fully functioning sales machine without knowing what you need to put into it in order to get the desired result out. You must know how people find your site, how many people click through to it, and how many of those clicks convert to sales. You simply cannot plan your long-term marketing strategy and predict your sales unless you know your statistics.

You would not believe how many people, when asked the question "How many people visited your site this month?" say that they don't know. You *must* know. If I can't get an answer to that first question, how am I going to ask the next, all-important questions, such as "Which pages do they look at?" and "How long do they spend on the site before they click off?" You really need to know the answers to all these questions and more. You need to know every detail of all activity on your website on a consistent basis or you cannot hope to improve your conversion rate. If you don't know your stats, you are simply relying on hope again! This is **not a recommended way to run a business**.

I have people coming to me for help who have spent upwards of £15,000 on a website. They want to know why they aren't getting any sales. I start asking these basic questions, that I've quoted above, about their analytics, and they have no answers. Would you spend £15,000 on a car and not know when it needs to be serviced, or what type of fuel to put in it?

You must know all the relevant information and how to analyse it. This information is the key to your success; you will use this information to plan and design your funnels.

Don't Rely on Opinion (Red/Blue Dress Test)

You can't base a campaign on guesswork and opinion; you must run an actual campaign to test and measure people's *behaviour* and use two variables to do so.

Recently, I was promoting an event and I decided to test a couple of campaigns to see which one would attract the most people to the event. I used two very similar photos of one of our female speakers on stage speaking to an audience. In the first picture, the speaker is wearing a **blue dress**. She has her face turned to the whiteboard so you can only see her face in profile. Behind her you can see a few students in the first row of the audience. In the second picture, the speaker is wearing a **red dress**. She is face on to the camera and she is smiling to someone in the audience (the picture is taken from the audience's perspective). She looks very friendly and welcoming.

Everyone I showed the picture to preferred the red dress picture. That was exactly what I expected because in the red dress picture, the speaker is smiling. Also, the picture is taken from the audience's perspective and the red dress makes her stand out.

However… when I *tested* these two pictures in campaigns, I was astonished by the results. I got almost double the conversions when I used the blue dress picture than I got when I used the red dress picture. Why? If you think about it in psychological terms, what does red signify? Danger! Conversely, blue tends to be a colour of business and formality… and authority.

I would never have known how people would actually respond if I hadn't taken the campaign through this **test**. If I had only gone on what people told me they *liked*, I would have wasted my money by using the red dress picture. After testing the two pictures, I put my money into the one that was going to bring me the most conversions, the blue dress picture. This is an example of how important it is to test and measure campaigns in order to work out which one you should put more money into. Take two possible campaigns and test them to see which one works best, test everything against a variable. Put your money into the one that tests best. Film studios often show test audiences two different endings of a film in order to see which one is preferred before they release a film.

Never make assumptions. I once made a sales video in which I said all the same things I was saying in my live presentations. The words I used were getting great results in my live presentations, so I assumed I would get the same conversion rates if I filmed my words and used the video online. I spent a lot of money on producing the video and uploading it onto my website. I then spent money on driving traffic to the website and waited. I got *no conversions*. I was mystified. Finally, I hired a video specialist consultant who explained that the video was too long. My offer was right at the end of the video and people were obviously clicking off the video before they got to the offer. I immediately saw my mistake. When you sell to people in a room, they are unlikely to get up and leave halfway through, so you can complete your message before you get to your offer. When you are selling to people through a video, they can easily click off it, so you need to get your offer in as soon as possible. The consultant explained how I could track the video, through the whole length of it, to figure out where people were clicking off it. That way I could ensure I put my offer in much earlier. It had never actually occurred to me how different those two channels were.

I made all the right adjustments, continuously testing the video, and eventually got the results I wanted.

The stories above are exactly why I love marketing; there are so many twists and turns, so many possibilities. All the testing and measuring makes it very creative. The whole marketing process is an art form, which is why it appeals to me as an artist – I still sometimes miss my days as an animator! And never forget that testing and measuring is an *on-going* process. What works today might not work tomorrow. You must test and measure *every* step of the sales and marketing process, on a consistent, regular basis.

These constant fluctuations are due to the fact that we are all emotional creatures. Every day we make countless different decisions and they are all intricately linked to our psychology. So we must have a very clear understanding of human psychology in order to make our businesses operate optimally.

4

The Psychology of Selling

Selling is all about communication, and communication is all about psychology. In this chapter we will look at how we communicate with each other, which is what we are doing when we are buying and selling. How do we use psychology in our communication and relationships with people? What psychological strategies can we use to help us sell people the products they need? We also need to analyse your psychological approach to selling and discover whether you actually *like* selling. You need to like selling, which means you need to like your product and know that people need it. Until you believe you are selling a product to people who genuinely need it you are probably not going to enjoy selling it to them.

The Sales Mindset

The main reason why most people don't make money in business is because they simply don't like selling. This is usually because they don't like being sold *to*. If you don't like being sold to, then you won't like selling to others. But think about it for a moment: why you don't like being sold to? Usually it's because someone is trying to sell you a product you don't need. When someone is selling you a product that you need, you don't mind them selling to you.

You have to get around any hang-ups about selling if you want to have a successful business. Whether you are selling yourself or your products, you have to enjoy the process of selling; you have to believe that who you are and what you have are of value to others. You have to get into the correct **sales mindset**.

We are born with a natural ability to sell. Once again, think about how you operated when you were a child and cast your mind back to the example I gave earlier, of the kid trying to sell the idea of getting a new bike to his dad. Every time you negotiated with your parents to get the things you wanted or do the things you wanted to do, you were selling to them. You also sold to your friends, selling ideas about games to play or selling your sporting skills in order to get onto a team.

So why and when did we stop being good salespeople?

In my opinion, one of the reasons we stopped being good at selling, or stopped liking it is because we became self-conscious and we developed a fear of rejection. As kids we tend not to worry as much about what people think of us, and for the most part we get over rejection pretty quickly. Say no to a kid and he might get angry for an hour, but he usually gets over it and moves on to the next request. Say no to an adult and they will agonise over it, over why you said no, wondering if it's something they did, taking it personally. Most of us are terrible at taking rejection and it hampers our progress.

If your product is good enough and you *know* how good it is, then you can't be afraid of rejection. Someone might not buy it, but you have to see this as *their* loss, not yours. If you know your product delivers, then you should not have any concerns about selling it. Again, think about when you don't like being sold *to*… it's only when the product is something you don't need, or doesn't *deliver* what you need. When you are being a sold a product that adds value to your life, you never mind being sold to. Most of us love Apple's adverts because we love our iPhones. We don't mind Apple selling to us. You have to believe you have something that people will love as much as iPhones. Use that mentality when you are selling to others. Make sure you are only selling to people who genuinely need your product, and ensure that you are adequately communicating this message to them. You must know *why* they need your product so that you can educate them on this.

So the key to selling is to have a really good product: a product that delivers and a product that you believe in. If you believe in your product you will be able to communicate its benefits to other people.

You also have to feel good about yourself. Selling is closely linked to self-esteem. If you feel insecure, you will not communicate well with others. Selling is all about communication. You need good, positive energy when you communicate with people about your product.

We all mirror the energy that someone gives off when they speak to us, so make sure yours will make people feel good.

Maybe you're not sure whether you like selling or not. Maybe you've never actually considered the question. Ask yourself now: do you like selling? If the answer is "no" then *don't* try to sell anything until you've fixed that, because you will be wasting opportunities. If your answer *is* no, then the reason is most likely that you don't believe in your product enough, or you don't believe it is good value. Only when *you* believe that you have an excellent product that people genuinely need, and that it is adds value to their lives at the correct price point, will you fall in love with selling.

Personally, I *love* selling! I love selling because I know that my products will massively improve the lives of my customers. The *by-product* of my sales is my profit, the money I make; but this is not what motivates me. If I was only motivated by making money for myself, I would spend my time trading the stock market and building an investment portfolio ... a much simpler and less exhausting way of making money. I want to help people; *that* is what motivates me. My products contain information that I know will change people's lives, so I want to get them to as many people as possible.

Unless *you* believe that your product will hugely **improve** people's lives, don't bother trying to sell it.

When people tell me they "hate" selling, I know it's not the selling process *per se*, it's the products they are selling. They don't believe in them. When they say that they hate being sold to, I point out that this is only the case when they are being sold products they don't want or need. When someone sells you something you genuinely need, that improves your life, you are grateful. If you truly believe in the value that a product will bring to a person's life, then you'll love selling it. You'll be *excited* about selling it.

The right mindset for selling means believing you are selling a great product to people who need it, knowing that your product will bring value to their lives.

The right mindset for selling means believing you are selling a great product to people who need it, knowing that your product will bring value to their lives.

What are we Doing when we "Sell"?

Selling is simply an exchange of **value**. When you exchange money for goods or services, you are simply trading two different items, two items that you and the other party have agreed are of equal value – usually a product on one hand and money on the other.

Back in the days before money, people bartered goods and services. I might offer you a sack of potatoes if you can spend an hour fixing my roof, or you might trade me a stack of firewood in exchange for me shoeing your horse.

When we sell products or services to people, we give them something of value in exchange for something they give us of value (these days, usually money). The more we exchange, the richer we all become. We add value to our lives as we accumulate more of the things we need, whether those things are material possessions, money, knowledge or skills. We all need each other's skills and products. I make products you need; you make products I need. I have information you don't have; you have information I don't have. The more we continue to exchange what we have and what we know with other people, who have what we *don't* have and *don't* know, the richer – in every sense of the word – we will all become.

No successful salesman starts out by thinking, "How can I make money out of people?" They think, "What do people need? What are the problems people have that I can fix?" Sir James Dyson always talks about how he is only motivated by "solving problems people have". Richard Branson became successful because he knew people wanted to travel to the US for a lower price than what British Airways – the airline that formerly had the monopoly on transatlantic travel – was charging, so he created Virgin Airlines. He then used his brand to bring people better trains, gyms, financial services and communication services. People got better services and products for their money, and in the process, Richard Branson became incredibly wealthy. Virgin is particularly good at finding gaps in the market. For example, Virgin "Upper Class" was designed to be halfway between the first class and business class sections on most airlines, giving people the option of travelling in the "best" class the airline has to offer for less than the usual price of a first class ticket.

I often meet people who tell me they are broke. They ask me how they can make some money. I always say, "Don't look at how you can add value to your own life, look at the value you can add to *other* people's lives." If you don't have enough money, reframe your situation and look at it this way: If you don't have enough money, you are *not adding enough value to people's lives*. Start adding value to people's lives, in whatever way you can, and charge them for what that product or service is worth to them, and you will automatically become wealthy.

Sometimes the value you can add to someone's life is *knowledge* in the first instance. A lack of knowledge can cost someone a lot more money in the long run.

When I first bought a BMW, no one told me that the tyres, which cost £350 each, need replacing every six months. This is because a BMW tyre wears down faster on the inside than the outside. I didn't know this. I soon realised that I would have to spend £2,800 per year on tyres. A tyre insurance company missed an opportunity. If someone had *educated* me about this and then offered me tyre insurance at the time I bought the car, I would have bought the insurance without hesitation. I would have been a **motivated buyer** ... but I did not meet anyone who had that information to sell to me, to tell me what I needed.

Remember ... give them what they want then sell them what they need. You motivate your buyers by **educating them**. What we don't know can cost us a lot of money.

If you don't have enough money, you are not adding enough value to people's lives.

How you Feel About Wealth is how you Feel About Selling

If you don't like selling, it could also be that you are uncomfortable with the idea of being wealthy. If asking people to part with money, no matter how valuable the product or service will be to their lives, makes you feel uncomfortable, then dig deeper into your subconscious to find out whether perhaps you feel uncomfortable with the accumulation of wealth.

In my first book (as I mentioned, co-written with my business partner, Vincent Wong), *The Wealth Dragon Way*, we explore in detail your attitude to wealth. If this is an issue that you know you have, I highly recommend reading that book as soon as possible.

Many people have been subjected to a lifetime of negative attitudes towards wealth, mostly reinforced by the people closest to them, such as family members. If people around you have always been saying negative things about money, like "Money is the root of all evil," then how are you going to view it in a positive way? You need to address these issues and become comfortable with being wealthy. This is not an easy transition; it is very hard to reject opinions that are coming from people you love, people who have cared for you all your life. But, as adults, it's important that we seek out our own knowledge and make our own conclusions. Once you're an independent adult you get to pick your own role models, so pick them carefully.

People who go around saying, "Money doesn't buy you happiness" are usually people without any money. I don't think I've ever heard a wealthy person saying, "Money doesn't buy you happiness." In fact, most wealthy people I know are happy and money has helped them to achieve that happiness. Of course there are exceptions, some people are clinically depressed, and tragedy can befall anyone regardless of their socioeconomic status. I've also seen people become miserable because the environment in which they make money, i.e. their work place, is toxic, so the *way* they are making money makes them unhappy. So money certainly doesn't *guarantee* you happiness but, in general, money can go a long way towards making you happy because it can buy you, and those you love, security and comfort. I don't think anyone could be *less* happy with money than without it. How they got their money might make them feel unhappy, if it was obtained unethically, or at the expense of another's happiness, but money itself never made anyone unhappy. And if you are genuinely not happy, money will give you more options and opportunities for finding out *why* you are not happy. Money may give you access to personal development that will transform your life.

There are so many negative myths around money. In *The Wealth Dragon Way*, we have a whole chapter dedicated to "busting myths" about wealth. For example, "Money is the root of all evil." I really don't understand where this comes from. Maybe it's because a few rich people have done some bad and corrupt things. But do you know how many bad things poor people have done? It's far more accurate to say that, "The *lack* of money is the root of all evil." A lack of money drives people to break into houses and rob banks, and even – at the other end of the scale – manipulate interest rates! Most of the people I know with money do really, really good things with their money.

If you are still in any doubt as to whether making more money will make you happier, then stop thinking about yourself and think about all the people you could help directly if you had more money. More money buys more food and that will *definitely* make a village of starving children in Africa happier! It's almost arrogant, or hints of laziness, to talk about money not buying happiness. Some people use it as a get-out clause. If you are fortunate enough to be living in a capitalist economy, in a free society, in a democratic country, with enough food to eat and plenty of opportunities, then is it not your *moral obligation* to make as much money as you can? Any you don't use for yourself can be used to help others. Is it not an affront to the people of the world who do *not* have freedom and opportunities to go around saying, "I'm not going to try and make more money because my granny always said, 'Money can't buy you happiness.'"

Look at it this way: if we can agree that money *can* bring happiness to people then we'll start to want to make more money. And in order to make money, we have to get good at selling. Eventually, this should make us *want* to sell.

We are complex psychological creatures, and it's easy to get stuck in an egocentric reality. In one person's reality, the struggle to get the money together to buy a cup of coffee is very real. In another person's reality, £5,000 is gladly handed over in exchange for a really good bottle of champagne. People find it difficult to imagine living in a different reality from the one they know, but we really need to step outside of our comfort zones. You must not fear what you haven't experienced, or don't understand, otherwise you will hold yourself back from new experiences.

As Marie Curie said, "Nothing in life is to be feared, it is only to be understood."

> Nothing in life is to be feared, it is only to be understood.
>
> —Marie Curie

Communication

As I mentioned above, psychology plays a huge part in how we communicate with each other. When you are communicating with your potential customers, language patterns are very important.

The words you choose, and how you choose to say them, can make or break a sale. An important word I often encourage people to use is "**because**". The word "because" can change the way your message comes across because it allows you to **qualify** your message. Think about a simple example. If you're at the back of a queue of people and you walk to the front and say to whoever is first, "Can I go before you?" they are likely to give you a simple, "no". If you walk up and say, "Can I go first *because…* otherwise I'm going to be late to pick up my two-year-old child from nursery," they will probably let you in. You have qualified your request.

The word "because" will often help you achieve your objective.

Conversely, some words can have a negative effect. Think of the word, "but" and how it can be used in many contexts. If you make a point to me and I say, "I understand *but…* " I am negating everything you have said. However, if I say, "Yes, I understand what you think *and* here's another point to think about," I'm adding to what you've said, not negating it, I'm actually *validating* your point so I'm not alienating you. Always remember that "**and**" is a preferable word to "**but**". It's more positive; it's a unit of conviction.

Units of Conviction and Resistance

In communication we have units of **conviction** and units of **resistance**. In every interaction you have with a customer, it's like you have virtual weighing scales measuring up your exchanges. On one side you have units of conviction and on the other side you have units of resistance. Obviously you want the scale to tip in your favour with more units of conviction so that the person you are communicating with feels you are on their side. If you're interested and want to study this topic further, read any book on NLP (neuro-linguistic programming) and that will give you a great introduction.

Units of conviction include a smile, eye contact, shaking hands, general etiquette like holding the door for people, picking up a restaurant bill, smelling good, wearing a nice watch, even the cleanliness of your shoes and your hair style. I've seen people wear a great suit, but with terrible shoes. The bad shoes just cancel out what could have been a positive impression made with the suit. Subtle make-up, if you are a woman, will be a unit of conviction, but too much make-up could become a unit of resistance. A man being clean-shaven is usually seen as a unit of conviction.

Colour is also important. The colour of your suit will determine how people view you. If you wear a bright yellow suit, they are not going to take you too seriously. A grey suit comes across as very cor-porate. Studies have shown that the optimum colour for a suit in business is navy blue. If you are a man, the colour of your tie is also very important. Again many studies have been conducted into this. A red tie, for example, makes people cautious (going back to the "red for danger" idea). Interestingly, there is evidence to suggest that, if you want to sell more, you should wear a pink tie. World leaders use experts to help them choose the right tie. How you look always affects how people respond to you. Even the degree of the shine on your shoes can make a difference. Shoes that are too shiny make people think of lawyers; shoes that are not shiny enough might suggest you are not as successful as you say. I'm not inventing this … there are global shoeshine consultants studying this!

But it's not just someone's physical attributes that have an effect on us.

Think of how the tone of someone's voice can affect you, and the emphasis they put on certain words. One person could walk up to you and say, "*Hey*," (in a lascivious tone) "Can I take you out on a date?" and make it sound like the most unpleasant and unappealing idea ever. Another person could say the exact same words "*Hey*," (in an upbeat, friendly tone) "Can I take you out on a date?" and the way they ask you makes you feel like you just won the lottery; you can't stop yourself blushing with pleasure as you accept.

If you want to see and hear a great example of all the differ-ent ways in which a single word can be delivered, you must watch a wonderful scene in *Toy Story*. Towards the end, Woody is trying to light a rocket that is strapped to Buzz's back so that they can go after Andy. He has a single match, no more; so only one chance to get it right. He strikes the match and it lights, but just before he can set fire to the back of the rocket a gust of wind caused by a passing car blows out the flame. His despair is palpable and he drops to his knees, simply saying, "No. No. No. No. *Nooooo!*" He says "No!" about 15 times, in different ways. There's the disbelieving "no", the angry "no", the despairing "no", the defiant "no" and so it goes on. One simple word, one syllable, said 15 different ways; it's not what he's saying, it's *how he's saying it* that makes each one so dif-ferent. That's such a great example of the power of tone of voice in communication.

I have an exercise I like to do with my students to demonstrate this. You can do it yourself if you like, right now! I ask them to say a simple sentence to the person next to them. The sentence is, "I want you to take responsibility for your life." I ask them to say it several times, never saying it the same way twice. I tell them to put the emphasis on a different word each time, or to take a pause in a different place. All these different ways change the meaning of the sentence powerfully. You can say, "I want *you* (pause for effect) to take responsibility for your life" or "I want you to take (pause beforehand for effect) *responsibility* for your life" or "*I* want you to take responsibility for your life" or even "I want you to take responsibility for *your* life" (as opposed to everybody else's life). Try saying this sentence out loud, placing the emphasis on different words each time and notice how this changes the meaning of what you're saying.

Or try this exercise ...

Tell your phone number to someone, the way you always say it. Perhaps you say it in three groups of numbers, such as "01234" (quick pause) "567" (quick pause) "890". Then write it down and get a friend to say it back to you using different spaces, such as "012" (quick pause) "3456" (quick pause) "7890". It will sound like the wrong number because you are hearing it in a completely different way. You have to hear your phone number the way you habitually say it or it will feel wrong. This exercise will show you how we get stuck in communication patterns.

When you hear information you are used to hearing come out in a different order, it scrambles your brain.

Always remember, it's not what you say, it's *how* you say it; just like it's not what you do it's how you do it. For example, I see so many people busting a gut at the gym. They show up time and time again, and they do the same work out, and they realise they aren't losing weight. This is because they are training the wrong way.

Change your training and you'll get different results. Change your communication and you'll get different results!

> **Change your communication and you'll get different results** ...

The VARK Model

We all have personal preferences, and when you are communicating with people, you need to think about what patterns *they* prefer.

Everyone is different; everyone's brain is wired in a different way, and if you want to sell someone something they need, it helps if you can figure out how their brain is wired. Work out what they need to hear and how they need to hear it in order to receive the message to best effect.

Some people are very visual, they need a picture; they will connect with a picture better than with words. If someone like this asks for directions and you say, "You go straight down to the bottom of the road, take a right, then your first left," they can't picture it. But if you draw them a map, they can probably memorise it, just by looking at it once, and get to their destination without any problem. Everyone absorbs information differently and you have to listen to what your customers tell you in order to find out what kind of learners they are. For example, if you describe something and they say, "That sounds really good but I'm just not feeling it," they are probably a kinaesthetic learner, meaning that they need to learn something by doing an activity.

After observing thousands of lessons, teacher Neil D. Fleming developed the "**VARK Model**". He suggested that, when it comes to learning styles, there are four different types of people: **visual** learners (V), **auditory** learners (A), **reading-writing preference** learners (R), and **kinaesthetic (tactile)** learners (K).

I could repeat the same sentence over a hundred times to a "reading-writing preference learner" and it simply won't go in, whereas an "auditory learner" will absorb it immediately. This is because the "reading-writing preference learner" needs to see it written down (and preferably even write the information out for themselves) before they get it.

Most of us have an element of "visual learning" preference in us. Human beings were participating in visual learning from the earliest days of their existence. We know that cave men communicated in pictures drawn on the walls of their caves, and ancient civilisations, like the Egyptians, used hieroglyphics (pictures) as an early form of alphabet. But as we have evolved we have developed different preferences in the way we like to communicate, and with more and more options, you have to be creative and aware in order to be a good communicator.

Body Language

Never underestimate the power of body language. It's estimated that verbal communication only accounts for about 7% of the information we receive. Another 38% is the tone of the words we hear. And 55% of what we take in comes from the **body language** of the person delivering the message.

If you ask someone if they'd like to do something and they say "yes" but their body is closed – their arms are folded, they are leaning away from you and they don't make eye contact – chances are they actually mean "no". When you are communicating with someone, watch for changes in their expression – a frown, or a tightening of lips or the neck – that could indicate that they might be feeling negative towards you.

You also need to think of your own body language when it comes to selling. Stay open; if you are closed, no one will want to buy from you.

Convincer Strategies

There are various ways of convincing someone to buy something. How someone operates, on a psychological level, will dictate which is the best strategy to use.

Because of their different communication preferences, people have different **buying patterns** that are based on their decision-making processes. You need to understand your customers' buying patterns to help you decide which of the following strategies you need to use, in order to convince them to buy the products you know they need.

Recommendation

Some people buy on **recommendation**. If they want to get someone to decorate their house, for example, they will ask a friend for a recommendation. If the friend says, "Yes, I know this person who's really good at painting houses … " then that's the person they will hire. If you find out that someone buys based on recommendation, make sure you find people to recommend your products to them! Get testimonials and present these to them. This is a very basic strategy and some people buy on recommendation alone. Other people are more complex; they may need a combination of recommendation along with one or more of the other following strategies.

Proof

While some people will buy on recommendation alone, others need *more* convincing. Before they buy, they may need **proof**. Given the above example, a person who needs proof as well as a recommendation would call the painter and ask to see photos of his or her previous work. They may even want to visit a place that they have painted to be absolutely sure.

Process

If someone needs even further convincing, they might want to see the entire **process** of the product or service. For example, most people want to see the "process" when buying a car. They want to see everything that the car does before they buy it. Of course the level of information they ask for will depend on their knowledge of cars. If your knowledge of cars is limited you might not know to ask certain questions about the engine performance. I know cars very, very well. Cars are my hobby, so I know all the right questions to ask to ensure I am buying the car I need. The price of something may affect whether someone needs convincing with the "process". Some people only need to be convinced by the "process" when the price tag is particularly high. Seeing the whole "process" could also include making comparisons between different products and comparing different parts of the process. Most people look at several cars or houses before they make a purchase. Again, the bigger the price tag, usually, the more convincer strategies are needed.

Scepticism

This is an interesting one. Some people actually use **scepticism** every time they consider buying something. We've all met these people; they are hard work! A sceptic will disagree with everything you say. You could say to them, "This is the best product in the world," and give them recommendation, proof and process, but they still have an overwhelming need to challenge you. How do you handle these people? Most of the time, you need to use all the above convincer strategies, especially proof, but after that, it's possible that they just need to be left alone. You can't push these people; they have to come to their own decision in their own time. With these people you almost have to become more of a consultative advisory seller. With people who are especially sceptical, you can try **reverse psychology** to test whether their objections are real or whether they are simply contrary for the sake of it. If you say to them, "Actually, I don't think this product would work for you. I don't think you should buy it, it's not really for you," and they start arguing against you and saying how much they *do* want the product, you know that their objections were not about the product itself but about their need always to challenge!

If you don't know what someone's buying pattern is, you have an obstacle to overcome. You will struggle to sell to someone if you don't know *how* they make their buying decisions. Understanding exactly how your customer thinks and operates is all part of the **psychology of selling**.

Unethical Selling

Unfortunately there are unethical salespeople who have given "selling" a bad name. This is because they have used these psychological techniques to persuade people to buy products that are poor quality or that the buyer does not actually need. This is another reason why many people have an aversion to selling or being sold to, they believe that "sales tactics" are bad. But we all use sales tactics; we use them every day of our lives as we negotiate our way through the day. The "unethical" element is not the *using* of psychological communication strategies *per se*; the unethical element is using them for unethical *purposes*. If you know how to break the code to a safe because it's your job to get into it if someone forgets the code, you are not being unethical by having that knowledge or putting it to good use when required to, you are only unethical if you use it to open a safe without permission and steal the contents.

There is absolutely nothing unethical about finding out that someone needs a product, can afford a product and using your selling skills to convince them to buy it.

* * *

Now that we have covered some of the fundamental aspects of choosing a product, effectively marketing it and ultimately selling it, we can move on to some of the latest ways that can help with this.

In the next part of the book we look more closely at how advancements in technology have disrupted and, for the most part helped, the selling process, including the marketing and advertising of products.

PART II

THE NEW RULES

The Digital Revolution

If you use the Internet (and if you know anyone who doesn't, it would be quite astonishing), you will be aware of the fact that almost *every* business in the world has an online presence. If you have a business, no matter what the size of your business, and regardless of whether you are selling an *offline* product or service or an *online* product or service, a significant part of your marketing, advertising, promotion and sales will now be done over the Internet. Only really big businesses these days think in terms of print advertising, and TV and radio broadcast advertising. Most average-sized businesses these days know that their money is best spent online.

I believe *any* product or service can be sold online, and in this day and age *should* be sold online. The more exposure you get, the more products you will sell; and these days **there is nowhere you can get more exposure than in cyberspace**.

The digital age has come upon us fast. There are people who are CEOs of successful companies who were born in the early 1990s and thus do not even remember a time without the Internet, or mobile phones or even Amazon! Almost every aspect of our daily lives now has a digital element. You can pay for parking using your phone. You can order take away food online. You can buy your groceries online and book the delivery of them online. You book travel online. You store your photos online. For most people, if you took away their phones and devices for a few days, they would hardly be able to function. I know I'd struggle!

And because *everyone* is using the Internet – to communicate, to socialise, to date, to make business arrangements – *you* have to as well.

It's no good saying you don't want to, or you feel you can't. You really cannot compete in today's marketplace if you do not use and fully understand all the online tools that are available to help you market and sell your goods.

If you are not familiar with how the Internet works you will get left behind. You must embrace it and make it work for you.

The Internet is an incredible phenomenon. In 1995, less than 1% of the world's population used the Internet. In 2014 that figure was 40%. It took 10 years (from 1995 to 2005) to reach one billion users, and then just five years to *double* that to *two* billion users. By the middle of 2018, more than half the world's population (that's over four billion people) were using the Internet.

We are going through a **digital business revolution** and if you are not part of it, you will be left behind.

> **We are going through a digital business revolution;**
> **if you are not part of it, you will be left behind.**

As I say, I firmly believe that any product or service *can* be sold online and thus every business *must* be online. You cannot have a successful growing business in the twenty-first century without a digital strategy, a presence on social media, and the necessary tools to navigate all the latest technology. You cannot communicate effectively and efficiently with your customers without these elements.

To start with the absolute basics, in order to run your company well, you must have the minimum tools. These include a good **Internet provider** with **fast broadband** or **fibre-optic service** as well as a phone package that gives you plenty of **data** while you're on the move. Obviously you must have a decent **computer** (preferably a **laptop** so you can use it at work and home), a **phone** and maybe even a **tablet**. You must also understand which **apps** (applications) can help your business (for example those that help with social media management or photo editing tools).

The digital revolution has massively increased competition. Business is very much customer-led these days. There is so much choice available; customers know they can get *exactly* what they want if they search hard enough. They don't have to settle for anything less.

Whatever it is they want, they know they can find it. If you are not providing it, they can find someone who is. So if you want to want to get noticed, you have to get very, very specific, with your products and your marketing and all aspects of your business. It is more important than ever to find your niche.

Anything can be Sold Online

Look around you. Anything you see can be sold online. Just make a list of everything you see. I look around me now and I see a coffee cup, a swimming pool, a dining table, a vase of flowers, books, a bookcase, some wine bottles, a leather briefcase, a suit jacket, a tie, a pair of running shoes, an iPhone in a case, a wallet… (I could go on!) Any of those things could be sold online.

You can take virtually any business online. You can be a florist or a wine broker; you can sell plants, fridges and even whole kitchens online. You can sell your landscaping services online. You can sell *any* form of consultancy service online. You can be an art dealer, buying and selling art online. You can even teach yoga online, having people join your online class over the Internet.

One personal trainer I know now teaches exclusively online. He joins his clients via Skype, on his phone, in the gym. The clients wear Bluetooth headphones and listen to him as he gives them instructions and motivates them. He can even multiply users, teaching five or six people at one time. This also reminds me of the "Insanity" success story. Insanity was a workout programme that was sold exclusively online and was incredibly popular when it first launched. It was marketed as the programme for people who haven't got the time to train; its unique selling point (USP) was that it could be streamed and completed anywhere in the world.

Everyone is online now. Dentists are selling their services online, vets are online, any service has to have a presence online or they simply can't compete.

You have to move with the times or you will get left behind.

Most people have no idea just how powerful the Internet is, or how much business can be leveraged with the power of the Internet. But just think about it… with more than half the world's population using the Internet, you have the potential to put your business in front of over four billion users, and to inform them of your products and services, at any given moment, just by guiding them to navigate to your page from the comfort of their own homes or offices. ***Four billion people*** could be looking at *your* website! It blows my mind when people say they can't find customers. There are ***four billion people*** you could reach, if you want.

On the flip side, think about the alternative … if you are *not* online, and your competitors are, then *they* have the opportunity of reaching those four billion Internet users instead of you. Is that really a position you can afford to be in?

Furthermore, think of the freedom you have when your business is online. If your business is open 24/7, because you have an online shop, then you can physically be anywhere. My laptop is now my office. In fact, with my current phone, the latest iPhone (plus size), I use my laptop less and less … you could say my *phone* is now my office! I conduct my business from hotels, airports, beaches, restaurants and conferences all over the world; basically I can be anywhere and I take my business with me. This is a massive revolution in business. My worldwide customer base is at my fingertips, around the clock, 365 days of the year! I have clients in every continent. And so can you.

Online to Offline or Online to Online

You can sell your products or services online whether they are *online* goods or *offline* goods.

An example of an **offline service** that you could sell *online* is dog walking. Many people need dog walkers. Obviously the actual service does not take place online, but dog owners will go online to search for dog walkers in their area. An example of an **offline product** you could sell online is furniture. Again, your furniture is not consumed through your computer, it will be delivered to your house after you buy it through the company's website, but the process of choosing it and purchasing it can all be done online. This applies to all offline products and services that are sold online, whether they are clothes, books, groceries or contact lenses.

An example of an **online product** that is sold online is a language course. You will buy the course online and probably receive all the literature and teaching tools through your computer, so the buying, delivery and consumption of the product all take place online.

Some products have an **online and offline element**. Ticket purchases (say for concerts or airlines) are a mix of online and offline elements. You purchased your ticket online and it might only ever exist in electronic form (even boarding cards are electronic now, for most airlines) – you might download the boarding pass or concert ticket to keep on your phone, so you never have a physical product, but obviously the *service* takes place offline. Indeed, the consumption of entertainment has gone through a massive shift thanks to the digital revolution, it's gone from buying DVDs and CDs online (that will be physically delivered to you) through to streaming services, so that you pay to listen or watch, but you never own a physical product.

Many educational services and products are bought, delivered and consumed entirely online these days. Any "how to" service is likely to be marketed, sold and consumed entirely online. If you do a search on YouTube for any "How to … " video, for anything from playing guitar to applying make-up, you will get countless videos to choose from. It's a massive industry. You can find videos on "How to sing", "How to date", "How to use an iPhone", "How to use Facebook", "How to use Google", and more. Many of these will be free, but there are also membership sites, like the one I set up to upload my videos on "How to negotiate BMV deals" all those years ago – although membership sites are much more sophisticated these days!

There are sites for pretty much anything you can imagine, for example websites and apps that are accountancy services, which allow you to punch in all your information and get your accounts processed. That's a great example of an online service that is sold online.

It's because you can sell almost anything online that I believe *every* business can and should be online. Any that is not is missing potential sales. With easy-to-use software and plug-ins, any business can take a sales transaction online, where the products and services are to be delivered offline or online. Hotel companies, shopping services, any consultancy service, recruitment agencies, even beauty services, can take bookings and payments online. Even businesses such as restaurants, where you pay after your meal, need an online presence for marketing purposes, even if they don't make actual sales online – although there are even apps that allow you to pay for your meal or drinks online before leaving the restaurant so you don't even have to wait for the bill!

The point is, as long as you have an **active website that is taking sales**, your business is open 24 hours a day, seven days a week, 365 days a year, with very few overheads. And if you don't need a physical space in which to conduct your business (as say a dentist or optician would, for example), then you have even fewer overhead costs … you have no rent (except the cost of your domain name and potential web developers), no office furniture to buy, or related services such as cleaning, and no security measures to maintain (a metal grille to protect your shop windows at night, and an alarm system, for example). Some commercial premises can costs hundreds of thousands a year in rental and other associated costs. Now you can rent a post box in a fancy postcode and yet do all your business online. Do we even need that? Most banking can be done online, invoices are all emailed and we are moving towards a completely paperless society. The more you can take your business into cyberspace, the more you save.

> **Anyone with an active website has an online business that is open 24 hours a day,**
> **seven days a week, 365 days a year, with very few overheads.**

Online Business is the New Normal

Increasingly, people are searching online for *all* their wants and needs. Even if you want to buy something from Ikea, most people go online first, because it's a good idea to browse and check that what you want is in stock at the location you intend to go to. People are doing their supermarket shopping online, they are booking vacations online; they are even organising their parties and weddings online and sending out e-vites instead of mailed wedding invitations.

Every business needs an online presence, at least a website, even if it's just a landing page that gives little more than a description of your business and some contact details. Even with businesses that might not seem like the obvious candidates for online presence, need to be online. Going back to the dog walking example, that I mentioned before, the point is that when people go looking for a dog walker, they usually look online first. They do a search online for a well-reviewed service, they find a suitable person who lives close by, they contact that person and book them, the person turns up and takes the dog for a walk and is then either paid in cash or online.

I still remember the days of a paper phone book. Can you even imagine? No one goes to the phone book anymore, they will go to Google, or at the very least log onto Facebook and ask their online community for a recommendation. If you're a dog walker, you can't afford not to be on Facebook.

If your business is not online, people will not make the effort to find you; they will find your competitor. You could be missing out on countless potential customers. There is a very simple saying that I encourage you to remember … "If you're not online, you're *offline*" – i.e. pretty much dead! You might as well kill off your business if it's not online. Even if you have a great restaurant, doing good business, people will expect you to have a website so that they can book, and a Facebook page and Instagram feed so that they can tag you. And don't forget, people love to "like" places that they like, so you need an online presence so that people can share their enthusiasm for you.

> **If you're not online, you're *offline* (pretty much dead!).**

By now, hopefully, you have embraced the fact that, if you have not already put your business online, you must do so without delay. But once your business is online, how do you get people to notice it? Your web page is like your "shop front" so you really need to get people to walk past it.

How do you get people to walk by?

In the following chapters we are going to look at how you get yourself online (which includes setting up a website and social media pages) and how you get people to notice you because, as you now know, it's not "who you know", it's **who knows you**.

CHAPTER 6

Your Online Presence

Until only quite recently, all you really needed, in order to have a presence online, was a website, or a few websites (maybe landing pages for different products on which customers could click through to a main sales page). These days, you really have to cover several bases, in terms of social media platforms, as well as having web pages that look good both as desktop versions and in their mobile-responsive version. If I click onto a website that is not mobile-responsive, I will click straight off it. And as I do most of my business on my phone, as do many people I know, it's *highly* important that your website is mobile-responsive. If it's not, go change it now or make a note to contact your developer immediately. You could be losing a huge amount of business.

Social media is also non-negotiable. Indeed, the first place most people will discover you now is on social media rather than stumbling across your website. **The social media revolution has completely changed the way businesses operate.** If you have a business, social media is not just an additional promotional tool you could use … it has become a vital part of any digital marketing strategy.

Some of your customers may still be finding you by clicking on Google ads, but many will now find you on their social media feeds, on Facebook, Twitter, Instagram and LinkedIn. Your website is almost your second tier of communication these days. It's still important because, while people may *find* you on social media, they will *validate* you by viewing your website, and checking that you are legitimate. If they find you on social media and try to click through to a website and find there is no website, they will probably not take you seriously. **You don't actually** *sell* **on social media, you** *market* **on social media and sell on your website.** But you cannot ignore social media platforms. They are the **new high street**, the place where your customers go to browse products and services.

Your Websites

The most important part of any business is having a place where people can find you and buy your products or services. You need a shop floor, and/or a *virtual* shop floor. When you market your business online, your shop floor *is* your website. Compared to how much time and money it cost me to build my website 10 years ago, what you can create these days, for very little money and effort, is incredible. These days you can create a website very easily and cheaply; and in many ways, the simpler the better. You don't need to put as much information on your website as you used to because you can spread it across so many different places. You can put your videos on Facebook, your pictures on Instagram and your corporate information on LinkedIn, saving your website as the place where you conduct your sales.

Your website serves many purposes. You can even have more than one site; you can have several sites in order to cover different functions. Amongst other things, your website is your calling card, your business's cyber-billboard. Whether you also capture data on it, sell products on it or share information on it, it is, first and foremost, your business's title page; your **digital shop front**.

If you are in business, you cannot afford *not* to have a website. You have to be able to reach your entire cyberspace marketplace.

As well as your main website, which should have all the most important information about your business on it, you can have additional websites to help you conduct business. You can use different types of sites for different purposes, e.g. for building a database, for launching new products and/or for funnelling traffic. The main types of sites that you can use, in order to find and attract motivated sellers, are:

1. **Authority Site**
   Your authority site is actually your **main company website**; its primary purpose is not to sell but to **inform**. Obviously you

will have a page or a link on this site that takes people to where they *can* buy your products, but the primarily function of this site is to give information. On this site, you will generally have several pages telling the visitor all about you and your company. Yes, you can spread a lot of this information across other social media sites, which is where people might go to look at it, but it should all still be available here. You will have tabs that take the visitor to, at the very least, a **Home** page introducing the business, an **About** page and a **Contact** page. If you have any media links you would put them on a **Press** page, and of course you need **links to all your social media feeds**. You might also have a Blog page. Blogs are particularly useful for SEO as they help your site to rank higher on Google listings.

The purpose of your authority site is to show **credibility**. You should have plenty of PR material and testimonials. You need everything positive that anyone has ever said about you on this site so that people feel you are well respected and *credible*. This is the site you should spend considerable time and money on.

You need a professional-looking website that has a menu bar across the top, several pages and, again, most importantly these days, a site that is **mobile-responsive**, which means that all the screens change to fit people's phones and tablets. With most people browsing websites on their phones and tablets these days, and that trend only set to increase, if people come across a website that is not responsive – meaning that they need to zoom in to navigate it – they will often just click off it, as I do. Customers are becoming increasingly ruthless; if they find a site hard to navigate they won't hang around. Hire someone who is an expert in the functionality of websites to help you. Even though some of the hosting sites and webpage building programmes are straightforward to use these days (most have a mobile-responsive feature built in, for example), it is still worth hiring an expert to build your website.

For any visitor, your authority site should quickly answer these three questions:

1. What does this business offer?

2. What value could I get out of its products?

3. What do I physically get from this company?

For example, if you have a company helping people lose weight, a visitor to your site needs to be able to find the information that tells them:

1. This business helps people lose weight.

2. You can achieve your desired weight loss if you buy the products.

3. You will get a 28-day diet plan and 24-hour support.

When I set up my website to attract motivated sellers for my property business, I made sure that they knew, as soon as they visited my site:

1. This business helped people to sell their properties quickly.

2. Completion could be achieved within four weeks.

3. Sellers would end up free of their properties.

You can keep your messaging clear and simple. People don't want to be bombarded with information or see huge blocks of writing, especially on the first page. It's better to present information in concise bullet points or phrases that capture the essence of the company. You don't need a lot of information on your main authority site, just bite-size pieces; enough to get the message across and give people an idea of what you do. It's more important to ensure it *looks* good. Again, this is simply your shop front, designed to entice people in. They will find out more about you and your products down the line.

2. **Value-Add Site**

Your **value-add site** tells your potential customer what **value** your product will add to their lives.

Ideally, this site will contain a **vlog** (video blog) where you can post videos offering significant content. You are not selling, *per se*, on this site. You can employ some soft selling tactics, such as some links to your products, but nothing that is too much of a hard sell. The focus of a value-add site should be to teach people something, so they know what you have to offer. When someone learns something new from you, something that *adds value* to their life, they automatically position you as an **expert**. So you could say that this site is also a **positioning** site. You are giving away a few free tips to encourage people to trust you. If you give away a weight-loss or fitness tip that actually works, people are going to come back to buy your products in the future. This site needs to be full of content that positions you as an expert; any visitors to this site should discover that *you* are the best person to learn from.

Think clearly and deeply about all the *value* you can add to people's lives. How can you quickly and powerfully give them a taste of that value, in a way that will qualify *you* as an expert? Use this site to show visitors that you are the best at what you are doing, that you know more than anyone else, that you know stuff other people don't know, that you are the best person to learn from. Of course you have competition, but you don't want your visitors to even think about looking up your competition, you want them to be so convinced, just by what you tell them on this site, that *you* or *your products* are the best, that they need look no further.

If you've given them value, you've got them engaged with you.

The fastest way to add value to people's lives is to **give them content that produces results**. If you give someone information on how to lose 10 lb in one month and when they use this information they *do* lose 10 lb in one month, they will trust you. They will come back and buy your products because they know that you give information that gets results. When people get results from *your* products, you automatically stand out from the competition.

> **Give them content that gives them results.**

You need to position yourself as an **expert**, and one way to do this is to be interviewed by someone reputable. If you are seen being interviewed by someone reputable (say the BBC or a well-known presenter), or an interview you do is published in a popular publication (such as *The Sunday Times* or *Forbes Magazine*) then you come across as an expert. All media links should then be posted on your value-add site.

You also position yourself as an expert when you are seen speaking on stage in front of an audience. Whenever you speak on stage, as well as having the opportunity to communicate with and impress the live audience in front of you, you have the opportunity to film the event. You can then use video clips on your value-add site to position yourself as an expert.

Ultimately, your value-add site has the dual purpose of **positioning you as an expert** and **giving away information that adds value to your potential customers' lives**. It doesn't need to be more than one page. You should be able to fit all the content you need, such as videos and downloadable information, and links to publications, etc. onto one page. All this content – your interviews, video footage of you speaking on stage, links to printed interviews, etc. – should position you as an expert *and* give visitors free tips. Your authority site can have several tabs for various pages, but keep your value-add site as clean and specific as possible, preferable all on **one page**.

3. **Funnelling Site**

A "funnelling site" or "lead capture page" is your primary sales site and is thus the most important website to get right. Your funnelling site is designed to sell your products to customers directly. These sites will use channels such as Facebook and Google to **laser target** specific groups based on many different parameters (based on constantly changing internal algorithms). You may find you need to use several funnelling sites because each site should be dedicated to a single product or service. The more products you are selling, the more sites you will need.

You also use your funnelling sites to **build your databases** because you capture people's details on them. Even though you will keep these sites very simple and limited to one page, you still need some content on them, some basic information. And you can include some added value, such as some video content, in order to give customers a taste of what you offer in case they have not seen your "value-add" site. But the main objective here is to sell products by funnelling people to your sales page, and ensuring you take contact details to build your database. You need to be careful to abide by Google's rules, though, because they can penalise you, even close you down, if they think your site is only for capturing leads. It has to offer some information, too. And you should always ensure you are abiding by the data protection laws of the country where you are operating.

If you get your funnelling sites right, they will dramatically improve your conversion rates.

You should have an auto-responder on any funnelling site, some form of **CRM** (customer relationship management system) software, to capture people's details and use them. There are several different types of software available. These software programs allow you to add a code onto the site so that every time someone fills in their details, it is recorded and added to your database. You can customise forms depending on what information you need. Of course, the most important contact detail to take is someone's email address, but you can also take phone numbers and physical addresses. You can also ask questions that help you qualify your traffic. You can start to get to know your customers' needs and motivations from the very first time they interact with you. Although don't ask too much at this stage. You might find that your conversion rate decreases if you ask for too much information at this stage. The simpler you can make it, the better. Don't over complicate it at this stage; you want to keep this site as simple and uncluttered as possible.

The best way of ensuring people give you **their real email address** is to offer a free gift of some sort. You can say, "Fill out your details to get a discount voucher" or "Fill out your details and we will email you your free e-book". If the free gift has to be delivered directly via email, they will enter their real email address! Don't forget to give them the option to opt out of you sharing their details with third parties. (And if they do opt out, then abide by it and don't share their details. Data protection is a hot topic these days!) Once they have entered their details, you can programme a message to pop up with words to the effect of, "Thank you. We have sent an email to you. Please click on the link within the email to claim your free gift."

The placement of your data capture form can also help to optimise conversions. Recent studies have shown that you generally get higher conversion rates when you put the form on the right-hand side of the screen, but this is exactly the kind of information that can change and become out-dated rapidly, so it's always worth looking up what the current studies have found.

You need a very clear **CALL TO ACTION** button that prompts the form to pop up as soon as it is clicked. Ensure your instructions are clear and simple.

There is some debate as to whether pictures or videos will give you higher conversion rates on your funnelling site. I personally feel that video can reduce your opt-in; I have always found that pictures rank higher when measuring my conversions. I have tested this several times in the past. If you feel that using video is particularly important, you must also track the video to check when people are clicking off it (like I did when I had an expert analyse my video, but these days you can get specific software that allows you to measure this, to show you where engagement starts to drop off). You can shorten your video or change it or move the call to action, and generally do whatever it takes to improve your conversion rates. Keep changing details and testing in order to optimise your conversion rates.

You must ensure that your funnelling page carries your own contact details. Every site you have should carry your telephone number and address so that people can validate you as a genuine, credible business. And make sure all your sites do look professional. I've seen many funnelling sites that do not. With competition increasing on an exponential scale, it is more important than ever to look professional across and throughout your online presence.

Many people ask me why a funnelling site cannot simply be incorporated into an authority site. This is because an authority site has too many options and distractions. There are too many places for a person to stop and browse, which keeps them away from the place where you want them, so that they buy products and/or leave their contact details. A funnelling site should have one, simple option … one form where you can leave your details.

And what happens if people decide to click off your funnelling site without leaving their details? You've spent a lot of money on that site and driving them there, so you don't want to allow them to leave without leaving their email. What you can do in this instance is programme an "exit pop-up" so that if someone tries to leave the site without leaving their details, a form will pop up offering them a "special one-time opportunity" and asking for their details. "Just fill in your details and we will send it to you." You really don't want them leaving your site before they have opted in, when you have spent so much money on marketing. This strategy can capture people who would have otherwise left your site. If they *still* don't leave their details, you can create a retargeting advert. You can install a piece of code that will make a pop-up window follow them around the Internet for a while until they do come back and leave their details.

Finally, I want to stress again that you *must* always follow Google's guidelines – that are constantly changing – or you will not be able to use AdWords to drive traffic to your site. The same applies with Facebook but Google is particularly strict. If you break the rules and get banned on Google, you may as well shut up shop and go home! Read all the guidelines thoroughly before running any advertising campaigns. If you don't play by Google's rules, you could get a "Google Slap", which means you are banned. This can be temporary or permanent. Google really does have the power to ban all your accounts and then you can never advertise with them again! People worry constantly about getting their advertising campaign on Google right, but they should also be paying close attention to what *not* to do.

4. **Launch Pages**

The purpose of a launch page is to introduce your customers and potential customers to a product or service for the first time. When you launch any new product or service, you should create a launch page for it.

My experience has shown that the best launch page will contain **four videos** telling the viewer the following information:

1. The first video tells the customer exactly what the product/ service *is.*

2. The second video tells the customer **what** they will receive or get to do.

3. The third video will contain *testimonials* from satisfied clients.

4. The fourth video will announce *how* to get the product/ service.

For example, if you were selling a new diet programme, your four videos might tell your potential customers the following:

1. The first video explains that this product will help them "**lose a stone (6 kg) and keep it off for a year**".

2. The second video tells the customer that they will have to "**drink three fresh juices a day for four days every week for a year**".

3. The third video is of people talking about **the results they got and how happy they are**. This may have a call to action offering an "early bird" offer.

4. The fourth video announces an **upcoming event that they can attend to learn more**. This fourth video contains a call to action and links to the funnelling page.

It takes a huge amount of work (and an understanding of psychology) to create the perfect launch page and produce the perfect videos, but it is worth investing in getting these elements exactly right because an effective launch page can massively increase your sales. Just think of the launches that Apple do. Think of how effective the videos they create are, and the campaigns they run. When the first iPad was launched, it was one of the most successful launches in history. They sold 300,000 in the first 24 hours. When the iPhone 5 was announced, they received 2 *million* pre-orders in the first 24 hours! Apple knows how to launch a product. In fact, if you copy everything they do, you'll be in with a good chance of having a successful product launch.

Prioritise your Funnelling Site

When you are allocating resources, your **funnelling site should be your priority**. In other words, this is the site you should invest most in getting absolutely right. I watch people spend all their money on a great authority site – producing a slick and attractive home page with great pictures and cool content, or putting all their efforts into perfecting their launch sites, but unless you have an optimised funnelling site, all your efforts will be thwarted, because the funnelling site is the one that physically generates leads (by capturing contact details and specific information from potential customers) and thus will create actual sales.

You will see many great-looking sites, especially as website-building products become increasingly sophisticated, but a flashy home page does not qualify the success of a business. Many sites that look amazing actually belong to failing businesses. That is because the pages of an "authority site" do not necessarily create traffic and generate sales. People are spending money on the wrong sites… they are misdirecting their funds. I have also seen people spend a fortune on driving traffic to their home page instead of their funnelling page. If there is no data capture form, i.e. nowhere for customers to leave their details and no immediate call to action, unless they are especially motivated to contact you, they will click off your site and probably not return. Customers have increasingly short attention spans; you can't afford to let them lose interest.

When people visit your home page or value-add page, they can easily get distracted by reading or watching your content, and while they might be intrigued, if there is no immediate direction to get them to leave their contact details, they probably won't take it upon themselves to contact you. You must capture contact details so that you can funnel potential customers through your sales machine or you will not maximise your opportunities to sell products. You don't want to miss any opportunity to take their details. You need those details so that you can continue to market to them. This is why you always want to spend the most money on directing people to your funnelling site, which will keep them focused on the one thing you need them to do at that point, which is to leave their details.

> **You must capture contact details so that you can funnel potential customers through your sales machine or you will not maximise your opportunities to sell products.**

Tracking

As I have said before, and I will say again (and again … and again, because so few people really take it on board) you **must track your results!** Unless you know what results you are getting from which set of parameters, you can't make changes to increase your sales. There are plenty of purpose-built software packages and tools that allow you to track your results, so there is really no excuse not to. There is no point in building a sales machine, in creating great websites, in making products and services that add value to people's lives, if you do not maximise your opportunities to make sales. There is too much competition out there and you *must* optimise your systems or you will not survive.

You must know your stats. At the very least you must know the following for every site you create:

1. How many people visit the site over any specified length of time?
2. How long do visitors stay on your site?
3. Which pages do people visit the most?

It's also useful to know where the people who visit your site are located. You can use this information to maximise your results by targeting areas where you appear to perform well.

These days, of course, it is not just your websites that you must track. A huge amount of your traction comes from your social media platforms. Luckily, most of them will provide you with stats automatically, and you can get apps that help you track activity on your feeds, but you must still collate and compare them when you try out different campaigns.

Your Social Media Platforms

Having a **social media strategy** is a core component of any business's communications and marketing strategy. If you are serious about your business you *must* incorporate a social media strategy into the very heart of your marketing plan. Whatever your business, you have to embrace social media and incorporate all the latest tools and technology associated with it. Your social media feeds give you *visibility* online; you must be *discoverable* online and the fastest way to achieve this is through your social media feeds.

If I walked into your company and asked, "What is your social media strategy? And is it at the heart of your marketing plan?" you should be able to give me detailed answers to those questions. If you can't, you need to address this issue urgently, because you can't compete unless you are where your competitors are, and your competitors are all over every social media platform. This is now at the heart of what I do as a business consultant; I work with businesses to ensure that their social media pages and feeds are relevant and effective.

Social Media is No Longer Optional

Whether you like it or not, if you are a business, engaging with people on social media is really not optional any more.

Only a few years ago if someone mentioned the term "social media", not everyone would even understand what they were referring to. These days, the term "social media" is a common term that is used in mainstream media every day. Everyone knows exactly what you mean when you say "social media". There are references everywhere: on the radio, on TV, in the news, in entertainment. It has completely overtaken mainstream media as the place where most people get most of their information.

Times have moved so fast. Until relatively recently, the heart of your online presence was your website. Now, a presence on all the major social media platforms is essential. Indeed, many people would argue that having a great Facebook page with a huge number of followers is equal if not *more* important than your websites. You can't really count followers on a website. To some extent, and for certain businesses, the same applies for Instagram and Twitter. You must have exposure on social media platforms or you will become irrelevant and invisible, and overtaken by your competitors. **If a potential customer hears about you and looks you up, but can't find you on Facebook, Twitter and/or Instagram, they will probably not take you seriously.**

Having said all of this, social media is changing *all* the time. Currently, Instagram is ranked as the social media platform with the highest engagement. But Facebook is close behind, and owns Instagram anyway. The world of social media is fiercely competitive itself. There was a time when Snapchat looked like it was going to challenge Instagram's meteoric rise. So Instagram went ahead and stole all of Snapchat's features (and made them better) and held onto its top spot. As with any business, the social media empires are fast-moving and ruthless!

If you are a business owner, one of your key priorities is reaching your clients and customers. You can't sell anything unless people know what you're offering. You can't wait for your customers to come to you; you have to go to your customers. So you have to know where they are hanging out. And these days, everyone is hanging out on Instagram and Facebook, so those are the best places for you to put your products in front of your clients. Again, you don't actually make *sales* on your social media platforms, but they are vital for customer engagement and marketing.

It's almost as if social media platforms have become our new high streets and coffee shops. These platforms are where people hang out and spend huge amounts of time; in fact far *more* time then they ever used to spend on the high street (because people are almost surgically attached to their smartphones and devices). Social media platforms are where we all live: browsing, navigating and communicating in a virtual world that feels real. Your customers spend hours, every day, scrolling through profiles and feeds. This is where your customers are. You must go there and make sure that you are part of their digital community!

Making your Social Media Feeds Relevant

Now we've established the fact that, as a business, it is essential to have a social media presence across all the main platforms, how do you ensure that your pages and feeds are effective and stay popular?

You have to get your social media pages *right*, which means posting the right content, at the right frequency, and staying engaged with your followers (in other words, replying to messages instantly). The first rule is that, when you create a page for your business on *any* social media platform, it *must* be about what you want to be known for. This may sound obvious, but I'm always amazed by the number of people who completely miss this simple fact. Like the example I gave earlier, of the calculator advert, I see so many people trying to "trick" people into engaging by promoting something that has little to do with their business. I see pages for personal training businesses that are only filled with content about travel. Or pages for people who want to promote their dog-walking businesses that are filled with pictures of people instead of dogs. You *must* stay completely relevant to your business. If your business is about parenting, make your posts about parenting; if your business is about fitness, make your posts about fitness. Do you have an art gallery? Then post about art … put your posts about holidays somewhere else. The content on your social media feeds **must be relevant**.

If you look at my social media feeds, on Facebook, Twitter or Instagram, you will be able to tell in an instant what I do. You'll quickly pick up that I teach people how to become successful in their chosen field; I motivate people. My pages are all filled with content about how to become more successful. I almost exclusively post content that is about getting more motivated. I would not suddenly post a picture of me playing and winning a video game (something I love to do!) Having said that, we are constantly seeing changes in social media and people want to know more the person behind the brand, so I do sometimes now post what I call "pattern interrupts" which are random pictures that are more personal. For example, when I took my wife out for her birthday for a very stylish high tea, I posted a picture of it on Instagram. Even though my feed is generally about my business, the picture got very high engagement because people were so intrigued to see something different, and it wasn't moving too far away from who I am and what I do.

You need relevant content because you need relevant followers. There has always been a saying in marketing that your "list is everything", meaning that your sales are very much dependent on the size and quality of your database – i.e. the number of people you can reach, directly, qualified by how likely they are to be interested in your product. If you sell dog food, anyone on your list who does not have a dog is pretty much a "dead lead". Now that we have social media platforms, it is your followers that are basically your "list", your **tribe**, people who know what you do, love what you do and want to buy the products you create. When you build a strong and loyal **tribe**, you have a group of people interested in what you sell, that you can reach *en masse* at any time.

Social media platforms are your *direct* channels of communication with your customers and followers. Look at every successful company, from Fortune 500 companies like Gap and Starbucks, to fledgling start-ups that have only just secured their first injection of funding, and you will see they all have one thing in common: a direct relationship with the customer. People feel empowered when they can engage directly with a company, like writing on their Facebook page or mentioning them a tweet. Of course you need to be very vigilant over what people are writing on your page (more about your reputation management later), but this direct relationship is vital for any business wanting to become successful today.

Find Out What your Followers Want

Earlier I explained how it is critical to your business to have a very clear understanding of who your target market are and what products they want and need. Social media platforms are a vital tool in this. Since your social media platforms give you such easy channels of communication with your followers, they allow you to find out exactly what your customers want. Remember the key to creating a successful product is to find out **what your market wants** and then give them *what they need.*

For example, when I was creating my course on building successful social media marketing campaigns, I went to my followers and asked them what they would like to learn about. They gave me an extensive list of topics and questions, including (and I'm quoting directly):

I want to understand what my social media needs are.

How can I get rid of my fear of technology?

How do I create more leads online?

I want to increase sales online.

Can I anticipate new trends through awareness on social media?

How do I increase my social media presence?

How do I get more mentors and investors through social media?

How do I launch a product using the Internet?

How do I use social media ads?

How do I get more followers?

How do I do email marketing?

Can I sell products I don't own?

How do I attract more clients and customers online?

How can I use marketing funnels?

What exactly is SEO (Search Engine Optimisation) and how do
I use it?

How do I get better SEO and VIDEO SEO? (How do I rank higher
on YouTube?)

How do I create landing pages?

How do I create digital online products?

This helped me tailor a course that would meet their needs.
When you are thinking of launching any product, you must first
ask people what they want, which will help you create the product
they need.

Before starting any campaign, you need to decide what campaign
you are creating. What do you want? What result are you looking
to get from this campaign? For example, if your initial objective
is to capture people's interest, ahead of launching a product, you
should probably run a teaser campaign. This is like a trailer for a
movie.

In a teaser campaign, you release a sample of your product and
encourage people to sign up to a waiting list for further updates and
news. Social media platforms are ideal spaces for launching teaser
campaigns.

Whether your campaign is a teaser, or a launch or simply
designed to increase your following, certain specific rules apply to
different platforms. Again, all this information is correct at time of
writing, but functions on social media platforms are being developed
and evolve all the time, so it's important to stay fully aware of new
tools as they are made available.

C H A P T E R

The Power of Social Media

Do not underestimate the power of social media! If there is one thing I want you to take away from this book, if nothing else, it is this message.

Not only do you have to get your social media footprint looking good, in terms of making your feeds attractive and interesting, and filling them with relevant content and amassing followers, but you must also be aware of how people are *using* social media. News spreads like wildfire through social media. It's almost instantaneous. As soon as any event takes place, someone can report it on social media; then everyone starts sharing it and talking about it. By the time the mainstream broadcast media is reporting it, it's almost old news.

If you are in any doubt as to how *powerful* social media is, the following story is a great example of how even the biggest businesses in the world are at the mercy of social media. The people have the power these days!

A Closer Customer Relationship

In April 2017, a passenger was forcibly removed from a United Airlines flight, apparently because it was overbooked. A number of passengers filmed the incident, which showed airline security dragging a man off the plane even after he hit his head and was obviously injured. Before anyone, at the company or within the mainstream press, had a chance to report it, everyone was talking about it, because the videos spread through social media like wildfire, going viral in a matter of hours. An outcry took place and many people swore never to use United Airlines again.

What hurt United Airlines further was their slow response time. Because they are a huge company, they presumably thought they had time to get their investigation done and their story together, but they left it too long. The damage occurred fast and ran deep, with United Airline shares dropping dramatically within two days of the incident. Many other airlines took advantage of the situation by flooding social media with positive stories about their care of passengers. This was a huge lesson for a massive company. Presumably other large companies made firm notes not to let it happen to them.

There is something of a tribal mentality on social media. People are herded along with the popular sentiment. This has always been the case in human nature, but social media gives the phenomenon a turbo boost! The harsh truth is that if companies fail to create a positive presence on social media, or don't engage with their followers instantly and carefully, they run the risk of being abandoned or ignored by customers. If an incident like the one that occurred on the United Airlines flight goes viral before a company can respond to it, a business is at serious risk.

We are all potentially subject to "trial by social media" and if an incident happens that might go viral and affect our public image, we have to jump on it immediately, we can never assume that the problem will just "go away" or fizzle out! **People across the world are staring at their screens 24/7. There is nowhere to hide and no time to lose. You have to stay ahead of the game.**

You must also be aware that social media itself is full of potential harm. "Haters" (people on a mission to sabotage anyone and anything) are everywhere and range from vindictive bullies posting fake bad reviews of restaurants to destroy someone's business, to truly viscous psychopaths getting their kicks from luring teenagers to commit suicide. You might not believe it, but it's sadly true. Recently there have been reports of these psychologically manipulative games that set teenagers a series of dares, the last one being to commit suicide! In Russia one of these games is believed to have led to the deaths of 130 teenagers. When you analyse the true power of social media, there are some shocking statistics and stories.

Unfortunately the Internet gives bullies and psychopaths (known as **Internet trolls**) the perfect shield to hide behind. Social media platforms are forever tightening their security, but people still manage to slip through the net by creating fake profiles and hiding their IP addresses. They are adept at avoiding detection and there are still not enough adequate laws to police cyberspace. It's all too easy to create these fake accounts and to delete them and start new ones when they are detected. What do you do if you have children? They are growing up in the age of social media; the Internet is an inextricable part of life so you can't ban them from using the Internet altogether. All you can do is *educate* them, so that they are aware of the pitfalls and know what to pay attention to, and how to spot and remove trolls immediately. Tell them about the dangers of interacting with strangers online and help them manage their online environment responsibly.

The same applies to companies. Business owners *must* educate themselves and take steps to protect their feeds from trolls while creating a wide-reaching online footprint. Ultimately, you need to stay up to date with cyber protection and data protection, and learn how to deal with trolls.

Public pressure isn't something new, of course, it's just that social media has become a vehicle that can massively amplify public sentiment and rapidly accelerate the speed at which it spreads.

An extraordinary situation unfolded in the wake of Princess Diana's death in 1997. There was a public outcry when the Queen didn't return from Balmoral (her residence in Scotland) immediately after Diana died, or lower the Royal Standard (the monarch's flag). It was nearly a week after Diana's death before the Queen made a public statement on live television after she finally returned to London. In this case, in the days before social media, it was the tabloid press that rallied public fervour with cries of "Where is our Queen?!" The palace had completely underestimated the massive public support and genuine love for Diana. It must be said, however, that the monarchy learned from this experience. Compare this case to the Queen's response after the tragedy of the Grenfell Tower in June 2017, where fire destroyed a tower block clad with flammable material and countless people lost their lives. The day after the tragedy, the Prime Minister visited the area but did not meet any of the victims, supposedly because of "security risks". Such risks did not deter the Queen, who visited victims with Prince William the very next day. The Queen was widely praised on social media, while the Prime Minister was strongly condemned.

Social media can work for or against you … just *never* underestimate its power to affect your business and reputation.

Here is one more example. In 2009 David Cameron was lambasted for criticising Twitter. In a radio interview he said, "Too many twits might make a twat," suggesting using Twitter was for idiots. Social media erupted over it. He had to backtrack rapidly and apologise for his comment. He simply didn't understand people's love for social media and it's huge power. Someone who *does* understand the power of social media is Jeremy Corbyn. Whatever you think of him, you have to accept that he really knew what he was doing as he campaigned the 2017 UK general election. He put social media at the heart of his election campaign and, as a result, many more young people than usual registered to vote.

Indeed, it feels like the younger generation are particularly empowered by their familiarity with social media. They have a place where they can make their voices heard and they use it. Look at the incredible way the relatively young high-school students who were the survivors of the mass shooting at Stoneman Douglas High School in Parkland, Florida used social media to campaign for gun laws. In February 2018, after they felt that politicians were doing nothing in response to yet another school shooting in the US, students took to social media to get their voices heard. And it was extremely successful. One student in particular, Emma Gonzales, who started the "Never Again" campaign has gone on to become a figurehead of the whole anti-gun movement, an activist known throughout the world. She regularly receives messages of hatred and even death threats, but her determination and courage remain undeterred. Within three months of the incident she had 1.5 million Twitter followers.

Managing your Online Reputation

The digital revolution is a double-edged sword. **While you have never had so many opportunities to make money, you have also never been so exposed.** One bad review could ruin you. You have to be vigilant all the time. You can't let up your observation of your online reputation.

Your online presence, or what is known as your **digital footprint**, will make or break your business. To survive, you need good reviews and positive messages on all your social media platforms and throughout the Internet. You must get good reviews on sites that are relevant to your business, where your competitors are getting reviews. For example, if you are in the service industry, you need reviews on Yelp and TripAdvisor If you are selling products (books, toys, make-up, food) on Amazon, you need good reviews on Amazon. The Internet is a ruthless place. A few bad reviews can ruin your business. You have to be aware of every single thing that's being said about you.

Online reputation management is a booming business as a result of the massive rise in Internet business activity. You can actually hire someone to monitor *everything* that is said about you online, and address any negative posts and report any trolling immediately. Even if you are just starting out in business, it's not a bad idea to consult an online reputation manager for advice at the beginning of your journey to find out more about what you can do to protect yourself. A lot of people wait for something to go wrong before hiring an online reputation manager, in a desperate attempt to clean up a mess. I think this is the wrong way around. It's like waiting for a burglary before installing a burglar alarm. Protect yourself *before* something goes wrong.

Nowhere to Hide

The Internet really is a totally ubiquitous platform. Think about it … most people these days (at least those who would be in the position to buy your goods and services) have a smartphone. They have the Internet in their pocket … all the time, everywhere they go. And yet many companies still behave as if the only way to reach customers is through TV and radio advertising, and the only way to sell them products is by getting them physically into shops. This is simply not the case any more. Unless you are a multinational company with money to burn, you can, and should, be focusing most of your attention online.

Being online is very exposing. The minute you meet someone and introduce yourself, they can search for you. Whenever I do a speaking engagement, I immediately get hundreds of new followers and friend requests. When employers are hiring, they do not just look at the applicant's resume, they check their social media profiles. Most people have a LinkedIn profile and plenty of social media content. Before you hire someone these days, you will automatically look at their online footprint. If I interview someone who seems really great for a job but when I check them out on social media I find their Facebook and Instagram feeds are filled with photos of them partying until 6am, it makes me think twice!

Anyone doing business with you these days will Google you. Mortgage companies will do a Google search on you before lending to you. Insurance companies will do an online search for you to ensure there is no evidence that your claim is false. Immigration departments will look you up. When my wife, who is from Malaysia, was getting her first UK visa, they looked her up on social media and presumably checked everything that had ever been written about her.

You have to be genuine and you have to be open. The Internet has made it virtually impossible to hide any information about yourself or your business. Customers and followers will not tolerate mystique or misleading information; it's all about transparency now. And it goes even deeper than simply being open; you also have to ensure that you are consistently projecting the **image** you are portraying, that you are presenting what people expect to see from you. You can't be officially promoting a healthy lifestyle and then post pictures of you eating at McDonald's.

If your image/brand is about wealth and you are teaching people how to become independently wealthy, you can't post pictures of you flying in economy. Lots of wealthy people *do* travel in economy, but if you are *selling* a wealthy lifestyle, you have to ensure all your posts, all your branding, is on point. We once had a guest speaker who sold himself as an extremely wealthy person. One of our students found his address on Companies House and it was a very rundown property. He got very defensive and insisted it was only one of several properties he had. He said that he was using it as a mailing address, but the damage was done and everyone got embarrassed by the situation. This might be a reason *not* to make your address public on Companies House – you are allowed to hide your address from the public!

It is very hard to build credibility but very easy to lose it, and it's even harder to repair your reputation once the damage is done. You have to be so careful. A couple hit the headlines in June 2017 because they appeared to be having sex in full view of other passengers on board a Ryanair flight to Ibiza while the man's pregnant fiancée was waiting at home for him in the UK. The woman involved (who, it was reported, has three children) was apparently mortified because she claims that it was just simulated and that they were having a bit of "drunken fun". However, the video went viral and she had to delete her Facebook account, claiming she was being hounded online, and that she couldn't stop crying because of all the hate messages she was receiving. Her reputation was destroyed in a moment of poor judgement. The man now claims his fiancée has forgiven him, but the point is that everyone involved was subject to "trial by social media". We see this sort of thing happen again and again.

Never underestimate the power of the social media!

Many businesses are completely unaware of how powerful the Internet can be, how it can change their fate in a heartbeat. Sometimes they find out too late.

Internet Trolls

Even if you do everything right you are still at risk from trolls. Internet trolling is a huge problem. There are new laws and regulations being put in place all the time but if trolls (cyberbullies) are determined, they will find a way to succeed in their cruel campaigns. Remember, as with all bullies, the cruel things they say are not a reflection of you, in that you mustn't think you've done something wrong if you get attacked, it's probably just bad luck. If it happens to you, you should probably hire a reputation manager without delay, as most trolls are experts at causing damage. I regularly use reputation managers for my businesses. But you still have to do your own work. Monitor people very carefully to ensure they are not trolls and never engage with trolls.

Having said all of this, I always tell my students that the flip side of discovering that you are attracting cyberbullies and trolls is actually that it's the first sign that you've become big enough to matter. In fact, the bigger your reputation, the bigger your footprint, the more they will come after you. No one is immune. JK Rowling is regularly trolled.

Remember, trolls are seriously disturbed people who need to attack others for gratification. Some of the comments they come up with are exceptionally awful. People who hit the headlines at the centre of dramatic stories are particularly susceptible. The parents of missing child, Madeleine McCann, have suffered terribly from online trolling for years, as has Amanda Knox, who was tried for murder in Italy and eventually acquitted. It used to be just sleazy tabloid journalists who could inflict psychological damage on people in the media. Now anyone can behave like a nasty, sleazy tabloid journalist and write terrible, false things about someone. And it's hard to catch them out because the Internet gives them both a platform and a shield to hide behind. Internet trolls are, unfortunately, a symptom of our times, and their tactics range from targeting celebrities with abuse to spreading false news stories.

You can, however, always challenge anything that is written about you online, especially since the European Court of Justice ruled in May 2014 that an individual has the right "to be forgotten" when personal data "appear to be inadequate, irrelevant or no longer relevant, or excessive in relation to the purpose for which they were processed and in the light of the time that has elapsed".

Identity Theft

Something you have to be incredibly careful about these days is cyber-crime. Before the Internet, the only things people could steal were your possessions. Obviously it's not nice to be broken into and have your treasured possessions stolen, but you can at least take out insurance so you can replace items if they are stolen. If you own a jewellery store and someone breaks in and steals £1 million worth of diamonds, you can recoup that. But how do you put a price on your reputation and even your identity? Cyber criminals are stealing people's identities every day. Several times, I've discovered that someone has set up a false identity, using my name and a picture of me, online. They are pretending to be me, and even charging people money for fake courses. Cyber criminals are very difficult to track down and prosecute. This is happening all over the Internet. Celebrities are discovering that their faces have been superimposed on nude photos and then those photos have been sold online. It's all very unnerving!

Having said all of that, sometimes it can be useful to give someone permission to assume your identity. The advantage of online communication is that it doesn't always have to be you, physically, replying to enquiries yourself. You can give someone access to your accounts and let them answer for you, pretending to be you, *with your permission.* This actually becomes a necessity as you increase your online presence and get more engagement – which is what you want, because you can't physically respond to every message yourself, you have to employ administrators and moderators to respond on your behalf. But you should still keep a close eye on what they are saying and doing.

Do *not* hesitate to protect yourself and be on your guard. The minute you see an account following you that seems to be behaving in a weird or aggressive manner, you *must* block the account immediately. Don't hesitate. Don't be shy or polite; be ruthless. Just block the account without engaging with it. If you engage with trolls you incentivise them to step up their bullying campaign because you've given the attention that they are craving. Act immediately to cut them off. Social media platforms give you the tools to protect yourself… you must use them. Once you ban someone, they can't see any of your interactions, even other people's posts where you are tagged, or post to your account again.

The Power of Viral Marketing

The best news is that you can harness the power of social media. You can use it very effectively in your marketing and sales campaigns. If you attract the right followers, your sales will usually go up as your following increases. If you post interesting content that your followers respond to, they will start to share it and eventually your posts may go **viral**.

I have a friend who has done extremely well thanks to the **power of viral marketing**. He went from 50,000 Twitter followers to a million in two years! It had taken him six to seven years to get those first 50,000, but once his material started to go viral, his following grew exponentially.

Viral means that people are organically sharing your content for you, rather than you purposely putting it in front of them. When your content is going viral, your followers are doing your marketing for you; it's like word of mouth marketing on steroids. Once something has been picked up and shared many, many times, people know it's got to be *really* good. When your content starts to go viral, it will be a huge boost for your marketing efforts. But this is only going to happen once you have a large number of followers.

What makes content go viral? This is the crucial question. It can be anything, but usually the key factor is that the content captures people emotionally. It could be funny, outrageous, terribly sad, or fascinating … it must simply stir people's emotions. Do your research and look at the type of content that generally goes viral. Think about why people share content. The main reason they do it is that it makes them look good to their friends; it shows their taste in humour, or their politics or their stance on an issue, so it connects people. Sharing viral content shows their friends that they are emotionally engaged with the world. Look at the type of content your competitor has created that has gone viral. Model your content on this but with your own products and services. And put your own original spin on it.

I'm a big fan of music and I've followed a number of musicians who have built their careers through the power of social media, capitalising on their material going viral. Korean singer JS Lee tried and failed to get a record deal many times. Eventually, he put his own music out on YouTube and ended up getting 50 million views. His concerts sell out. He doesn't even need a promoter. Jason Chen is a US-based musician who has built his success on YouTube simply by doing covers of other people's songs. He also now has 50 million followers. He includes a link to iTunes on his videos so that his music sells. Sungha Jung, another Korean musician, also does covers. He doesn't even sing, he just plays guitar incredibly well. He did a cover of the Jason Mraz song, "I'm Yours". Jason heard it and invited Jung to play live on stage at one of his concerts!

Having said all this, going viral never *guarantees* financial success. You still need to know how to monetise your popularity. This is something we will look at in a subsequent chapter on creating a business out of your brand (basically monetising your following). Building a following on social media is important, but you still have to know how to harness that potential power. I know of people with a million followers on Twitter or Instagram who are still broke because they have no idea how to turn that popularity into a successful business.

First, let's look at how you create the social media campaigns that will help you build your following.

8

A Guide to Building Successful Social Media Campaigns

In this chapter I want to give you a very clear, practical guide to creating campaigns for each of the major social media platforms that are most popular at time of writing.

There are endless social media platforms and new ones are being created all the time. Social media started with platforms such as *Friends Reunited* and *MySpace*. Those were the platforms that started the trend and that were popular 10 years ago. Today, in 2017, these early platforms have been eclipsed by the major players. If you want to stay ahead of the competition in business, you must have a presence and an effective campaign on each of the following major six platforms. To remember the list (although we will discuss them in order of importance, rather than this order, below), I use the acronym FLY GTI, which stands for:

Facebook
LinkedIn
YouTube
Google (in other words a Google account and Google+ account)
Twitter
Instagram

These are the main six platforms that, at the time of writing, I believe are essential – in other words, not optional – for your business. There are many other platforms and apps available, such as blog host Tumblr (owned by Yahoo! and according to statistics at time of writing hosting over 400 million blogs and attracting 555 million monthly visitors) and messaging application Snapchat (with its 166 million daily active users, according to statistics published at time of writing), but I think these are optional rather than essential. Use whichever additional platforms you like and feel are relevant to your business, but you really *must* use the six platforms and channels I identify here as your core platforms. You must furthermore understand and use *all* their available tools and functions. Why? Because everyone else is. You can't afford to ignore any of them. You can't say, "Oh, I really get and love Facebook but I don't bother with Twitter because I hate it," because you will be missing out on opportunities that your competitors are taking advantage of. You will be missing business opportunities. Can you afford to do that? Moreover, you will be judged on it. When customers don't find you across all social media platforms, if you do not have a full social media presence, they will mark you down for it.

Every platform has its own style and tools for building a successful marketing campaign, but they all have the same important function: these platforms are how you attract followers, where you build your tribe, your all-important *list*. What used to be a list of email addresses on a database is now your following across your social media platforms.

Social media platforms are now absolutely vital to your business success. Whether you like them or not, you *must* embrace the fact that they are here to stay, that they are the central part of most of your customers' lives, and that by capitalising on their power you can massively grow your business. They are the main channels through which you reach the online communities.

Facebook

Facebook has become possibly the most important social media platform of all time. The site started by Mark Zuckerberg in 2004 as a forum for connecting Harvard students, similar to *Friends Reunited*, has grown exponentially to outperform all its competitors. Facebook reached its first billion users at the end of 2012, having grown from 100 million in 2008. By the middle of 2017, Facebook had over **two billion users worldwide**.

There are several different ways in which you can appear on Facebook. Initially, you can obviously have a **personal profile**. You can also set up a **group** and invite people to join based on a specified interest. And, perhaps most importantly, you can have a **business page**, or a **fan page**. Facebook Pages have become essential for businesses on a local and global scale, and a key channel for B2C (business to customer) communication.

Facebook gives you all the functions your "authority site" (as I described earlier) performs, in that it gives people a place where they can find out relevant information about your business and get regular updates about what you are doing. As a business, your Facebook page has become equally as important – if not more important – as your main authority site. Of course you still need your authority site, for credibility, but you need a Facebook Page, too. If you don't have a Facebook Page for your business, I believe it will hurt your business.

One of the main advantages of a business page is that you can have unlimited followers and "likes" (whereas your personal profile limits your friends to 5,000). In addition to a business/fan page, you can use a Facebook "group" that allows you to build a list of people who are interested in a particular topic, but these are more about the members connecting with each other. Using your Facebook Page, every time you launch a new product or service, you can immediately market it to an established community of potential customers who have already declared their interest in the relevant market.

Keeping your Facebook Page Current and Relevant

Your strategy for your Facebook Page should be focused on keeping people up to date with what you are doing, to keep you and your business in people's minds. Your fan page is not the place to put lots of pictures of you partying with your friends. A few personal photos (especially if they enhance your business profile) are fine, but choose them very carefully. For example, I put a few a pictures of my wedding on my fan page, and when I travel I post pictures of me and my wife or business partner enjoying luxurious hotels in exotic locations, as well as pictures of us travelling in business class and using executive suites, because my business has a focus on creating that kind of lifestyle. I try to post a few casual photos, too, to make me relatable, but nothing that would detract from my business profile. For example, I wouldn't post pictures of, or references to, my video gaming hobby on Facebook, as it wouldn't fit with my business profile.

Facebook is a more effective way of reaching people with your campaigns than the old style mailshot to your email list. For a start, it's more visual and feels more personal. In my experience, people are happier receiving marketing material on their Facebook feeds than they are being bombarded by marketing emails. If you have 50,000 people's email addresses and you bombard them with emails every day, they could easily get annoyed because they feel personally targeted. Also, it's all too easy to filter emails off as spam, or not open them and read them. Facebook puts your ad in front of your potential customers in a subtler, less aggressive way; it allows you to market to your potential customers in a way that does not seem so intrusive.

Building your Following

Finding new followers is also made easy for you by Facebook. There is a function that enables you to link your Facebook account to your email account so you can see if there are any matches. Facebook can scan your email list and let you send a friend request or a "like this page" invitation to anyone on it.

Facebook is one of the simplest and most straightforward platforms to use. It is easy to laser target your audience and filter people out based on their preferences. Users give a huge amount of information about themselves on their Facebook profiles, which businesses can use to help them target relevant audiences. You can also use relevant Facebook groups to build your following and market your product by approaching the admin people of the group and asking them to promote your business. You can target niche groups that are specifically relevant to your product or service.

My top 10 tips for getting Facebook engagement are:

1. Post regularly.
2. Ask people for their opinion.
3. Ask your audience questions.
4. Run competitions.
5. Run at least two Facebook Lives per week.
6. Post something controversial.

7. Reply to everybody's comments.

8. Like everybody's comments.

9. Post "light" images (i.e. lots of white and light colours rather than black/dark).

10. Tell a personal story then ask people if they relate to it and ask them to share their similar stories (video works well for this).

Facebook Ads

Facebook has built its own advertising platform. Facebook Ads have become hugely important in the business world. The feature can be a little daunting at first, and complex to use, so you should consider taking a course to learn all the specific techniques to get it right, but Facebook Ads are a great way of filtering users and targeting your ideal customers.

Facebook's marketing functions are incredibly sophisticated. You can choose to market to certain target groups based on a whole range of parameters, such as location, interests and the user's browsing history. Facebook then disguises your ad as a "suggested post" or a "sponsored post", which makes it less intrusive. For example, if I've got a property event in London, I can target users in London who have been doing property related searches. Or if I'm marketing a book about personal development and asset building, I can target all users who follow Anthony Robbins or Robert Kiyosaki, two of the best-known authors in those fields. I can instruct Facebook to post my ad on the profile of anyone who has liked either of these authors.

You have to learn how to filter your audience. You start with a small budget and test the ad to see if you get results (remember, we test and measure *everything*). If you don't get the results you want, you change the ad. If you do, you scale up and assign a bigger budget. If your ad continues to convert people, scale it up again. It's all about ensuring your filters are working, and checking that the ad is reaching the right people, but you have to get the economics right. When you pay for an ad, you want to make sure you make back more than you have spent, as with examples I gave in the first part of the book. It really doesn't matter what you spend (or, more accurately, *invest*) as long as you make more than you spend. Test your targeting by trying out different ads to see which ones give you the most conversions.

With its two billion users worldwide, Facebook has become a huge marketplace! If you are not using Facebook to market your products, you are missing a massive opportunity, and you will not keep up with your competitors. However, as with all marketing strategies and online services, if you don't know what you are doing, you could lose money fast. You *must* learn exactly how to maximise your results or you will burn through your budget rapidly, with very few results. Your money is best invested, in the first instance, on educating yourself. You must learn how to use Facebook ads effectively. You can either invest money in educating yourself or lose money as you learn how *not* to do it. The choice is yours!

Facebook Live

Facebook Live is an example of a fairly recent new feature that has been launched by the company, and it has fast become an incredibly powerful tool. It allows you to broadcast to everyone in your network *and* in your friends' networks. Anyone who follows you, as well as any of their friends, will be able to view your videos, live, and replay them once you've finished broadcasting.

When Ariana Grande gave a tribute concert in 2017 for victims of the devastating Manchester Arena bombing that had happened at her concert two weeks previously, it was streamed on Facebook using Facebook Live and apparently had over 76 million views. It's estimated that over 22,000 people donated money as a direct result of this streaming.

In the summer of 2016, some of the Olympics events went out on Facebook Live. I remember sitting in a Starbucks in South Korea watching the finals of the Badminton, (a sport I follow and am passionate about) that were taking place live in Rio via Facebook Live. One of the best features of Facebook Live is the function that allows you to "like" and post comments on the video in real time. I loved commenting and connecting with fellow fans as we cheered on our Malaysian hero, Lee Chung Wai, to his silver medal (and commiserated with each other when he narrowly missed out on winning the gold). Because we were able to connect with each other in real time, it really was like we were all there.

Mark Zuckerberg himself has been using Facebook Live to promote **Oculus VR**, the company's new virtual reality platform.

An additional bonus of Facebook Live is that, if you build a big network of followers, you can let someone with a related business to yours "lease" your page. For an agreed fee, you can give them admin control on your business page and permission to post their Facebook Live feeds in order to broadcast live to your followers. You are, literally, renting out your space. The flexibility you now have within Facebook Live is incredible. I can target exactly the right people, and even sell within my video by inserting links or by pinning links to comments. Everything that you recorded live, including the comments that were made at the time the video was broadcast, will be recorded and can be replayed any time.

With all its advancements in video posting technology, Facebook is also making great strides in challenging YouTube's share of the viral video market. Recently they have been actively encouraging people to upload video content straight to Facebook, bypassing the YouTube stage, so that it becomes embedded in your Facebook feed rather than only be accessed through the YouTube link the post is attached to.

I believe the success of features such as Facebook Live, indeed the very success of Facebook and other social media platforms, is due to the fact that, ultimately, we all crave connection. Even though we are all "glued" to our phones and computer screens, for the most part we are not interested in a solitary experience of life. We *want* to be connected to other people. Social media helps us do that to an even greater extent than in real life (because we can reach people anywhere on the planet at any time). We are all constantly searching for our communities and tribes. Social media really does keep us together; it helps us connect and share our opinions; it gives us a sense of belonging.

Twitter

Twitter started its life in 2006. The idea, initially, was to offer users a way of creating short SMS-style messaging online. Although it has grown massively in terms of the numbers of people using it, Twitter is still basically just a simple feed that restricts users to 280 characters per posts, although many users these days get around that by posting multiple times in instalments (labelling them as 1/12, 2/12, 3/12 and so on until they have formed a longer message).

From its modest beginnings, within 10 years, Twitter grew to having more than 300 million users. At the time of writing, while Twitter is a relevant and essential part of any ambitious business's communications strategy, the platform is not quite the powerful *sales* platform that Facebook and Instagram are (granted, you don't sell *on* Facebook and Instagram, but you do promote specific products and provide call-to-action links to take people to where they can buy products). Twitter is more effective as a general marketing tool; it is excellent for raising your profile, and getting information across and educating your target audience. Twitter allows you to talk to your followers like they are your friends. You can have direct conversations with individuals, which is what people like and expect these days. There is no room for extraneous formalities on Twitter. Because of the 140-character restrictions, messages tend to be colloquial, direct and usually on point.

Twitter has dramatically changed the public's relationship with famous people; it has removed all the traditional barriers that stood between "regular people" and "celebrities". Famous people, who used to be viewed as unreachable, have Twitter accounts, and people can communicate with them directly. Even key members of the Royal Family have Twitter accounts. And unless you have been under a rock for a couple of years, you will know that the President of the United States has a Twitter account (whether or not this is a good or bad thing is a matter of opinion). These people used to be shrouded in mystery. Nowadays people *expect* to be able to connect with whomever they want. We see celebrities tweeting very personal pictures and information. They comment directly on their personal dramas and scandals. Where there was mystery, now there is absolute transparency. Anyone who isn't transparent, or tries to pull the wool over their fans' eyes, is quickly found out.

Twitter for Marketing

Twitter is a great tool for marketing, especially when it comes to targeting people with relevant interests. You can run **Twitter Adverts** in a similar way to the way Facebook works. Twitter will place adverts – calling them "Sponsored Tweets" – in front of exactly the right people according to the preferences you choose. Twitter algorithms are excellent at filtering users and finding the right people to target. For example, if I'm writing a book that I believe Richard Branson's followers will like, I can pay Twitter to put a sponsored tweet in front of all Richard Branson's followers. The cost of doing this is not as expensive as you might imagine.

The technical aspects of running ads change constantly and you should always keep up with the latest changes being released by Twitter, and indeed all these platforms.

Instagram

In the same way that Twitter is a sort of condensed version of a Facebook status update (with the 140 character limit), Instagram hones in on one aspect of our appetite for sharing content: the posting of photographs and videos. The emphasis is on the visual not on the text, although hashtags can be added to help people find posts related to their interests and, again, Instagram has become an important platform on which people can communicate with celebrities and businesses.

Of all the platforms, Instagram perhaps feels the most personal and intimate because we are *seeing* quite personal content, but it can still be used as a business marketing tool if you post relevant content. It is a particularly strong tool for helping to build your brand. Followers can easily see what you are about because your content is so visual. Instagram is a little more indirect as a marketing tool, it is almost an "indirect" marketing tool because your content will not be too sales-focused or formal.

That said, ignore Instagram at your peril because it is becoming one of the highest *engaged* platforms in the world, if not *the* highest.

The most important rule for posting on Instagram is to keep your content **relevant**. You can mix up styles and moods, but you should always stick to the same theme. As I've said before, don't post fitness pictures on an Instagram account for a dog-walking business, or holiday snaps on an account for a food brand (unless they are related to the type of food associated with your brand in some way). At time of writing, I would recommend posting around three times a day and using only five to seven hashtags. If you use more hashtags than this, it can look like spam and Instagram won't show the post to your followers as often as it could. But algorithms are changing all the time, so keep testing and measuring. Recently, we've seen a huge surge in engagements when location tags are used, both in posts and within "Insta-stories", so the current advice is … always tag your posts with a location.

With Instagram you should give your posts a more personal/casual feel than Facebook, or even Twitter, because that is what users expect. Make it more of a soft sell. Keep your product in the background – although do feature it!

In the wake of being bought by Facebook, Instagram has had a big overhaul of its features. For example, to compete with Snapchat, Instagram introduced the "My Story" feature, which allows you to post a short video that is available to your followers above their feed, and on your home page. After 24 hours, the video is deleted.

You can also advertise in someone else's feed or story by inserting a call to action. For example, I could tag someone in one of my posts in order to drive *my* followers to their account. People will pay you to do this according to how many followers you have. This is one way of monetising your following, as we will come on to discuss in more detail later.

YouTube

In my opinion, the next most important platform you need a presence on – after Facebook, Twitter and Instagram – is **YouTube**. The video-sharing platform has exploded in recent years; it is becoming the heart of the viral world and a real challenger to regular television. But it is not just as a content-sharing platform that YouTube has disrupted the market, it has also become the second biggest search engine in the world after Google (whose parent company owns YouTube anyway). There was a time when people generally arrived at YouTube though links on other web pages, or through social media platforms. People are increasingly using the YouTube platform itself to conduct searches, so it has become a significant platform on which businesses must advertise. The younger generation in particular practically live in a YouTube universe!

YouTube is especially relevant in music and entertainment but it has become *most* popular for the "How to … " videos that people post. Over half the searches on YouTube are for "How to … " videos. These videos give you the ideal opportunity to put your products in front of a highly targeted audience. If you are selling organic coffee and you find a YouTube channel dedicated to coffee drinkers, with "How to make the perfect cup of coffee" getting millions of views, where better to place your advert for organic coffee? This would be a much better place to spend your money than a spot during a television show when you have no idea how many coffee aficionados will see it, and certainly have no accurate way of measuring your results. When you put your advert in front of a video teaching people how to make the perfect cup of coffee, you can be pretty sure just about every single person watching that video is going to be an avid coffee drinker! YouTube also allows you to measure your results so you always know how many people have watched your video and how long they watched it for.

YouTube has many features for placing advertising. One option is to interrupt people while they are watching a video. At a particular point in the video, the viewer is interrupted by an ad of around 10 seconds that you cannot switch off without going back to the beginning of the video. This is pretty aggressive advertising but it is not much different from watching regular television when adverts interrupt your viewing, although it does get around the fact that people can skip through adverts when they record TV shows to watch back at a later date.

A more popular and less aggressive option is to use pre-adverts. This is what many advertisers use. Almost every time you go to watch a YouTube video these days, you will see an advert for at least five seconds before you are given the option to "skip ad". These are highly effective but need to grab the viewer's attention in those first five seconds to keep them engaged otherwise they will click off it. Some adverts do not have the "skip ad" feature. Most film trailers, for example, have pre-adverts on them that you can't skip. Similarly most music videos these days will have ads that play at the start. This creates revenue for the creator of that content.

If they allow advertising content, the creators (or owners) of the YouTube videos you advertise on will be paid every time someone clicks on an ad. Alternatively, you can negotiate to pay them up front. Some creators will not allow advertising on their YouTube videos but most do, since it is a significant source of income for them and the main reason some of them are posting content in the first place.

To the best of my knowledge, the YouTube video that has had the most views in history is the original "Gangnam Style" video by PSY. It had so many hits, YouTube reportedly had to add an extra digit to its views counter. Previously, the counter only had 9 digits. When Gangnam Style was close to receiving its 999,999,999th view, they had to add another digit so that the counter could register 1,000,000,000 views! Originally posted in July 2012, the video hit *three billion views* in November 2017. Can you imagine that many people seeing your ad in a relatively short space of time? Where and how else could you make that happen? If you had been running an ad on that video since it was first posted, three billion people would have seen your ad! Find the next "Gangnam Style" and you're made!

Posting an advert on other people's videos is highly effective, especially if the YouTuber has a high number of followers. If you discover a video on YouTube that you think will be watched by the kind of people you would like to market to, and that person allows advertising on their video, find out if you can post your ad on their video. Look for videos that are getting a high number of views. If I'm marketing a book on a certain subject, I'll look for relevant YouTube videos and place ads on those videos. My ad will come up as an overlay on the video with a pop-up box that invites the viewer to click through to my website. This is the most important part. There's absolutely no point in running an ad on YouTube if you don't have a clear "call to action" button. People are unlikely to stop what they are doing to search for you and find their own way to your website. You are competing for people's attention every minute of the day; you have to make it easy for them or you will lose them.

There is so much competition on YouTube these days, and the range of videos available is vast, so you can be very selective over which videos you advertise on. You will find videos that look very professional and more amateur-looking ones, but don't discount the latter. You can't assume that more professional-looking videos automatically get more hits. Sometimes it is the amateur ones that get more hits because they are more authentic and viewers can relate to them. We've all seen the kind of videos that go viral. The most popular ones tend to be very off-the-cuff candid videos, the ones that come across as being very authentic, often with people or animals caught doing hilarious or adorable things. In 2007, a father caught his sons, one-year-old Charlie and three-year-old Harry in the most adorable video clip in which Charlie bites Harry's finger harder than the older brother had been expecting. The video went viral and since then has been watched over 800 million times! The majority of professionally produced videos have had nowhere close to that number of views. No one could have predicted the runaway success of this little home video.

When you are looking for content to place your adverts on, do your research on which videos, in the markets that are relevant to your products, tend to go viral the fastest. You should also be aware of this when you are creating your own content. Think carefully about whether, for your business, a professional-looking or more intimate-style video would work best. If you can, make two and test them against each other. Remember, we always test and measure, at every stage.

LinkedIn

If you are a business owner and/or providing a professional service, you must have a **LinkedIn** profile. Even if you don't use LinkedIn as a platform to post on regularly, you should be visible on it, and – depending on your business – use it to network and make business connections.

Launched in May 2003, by the middle of 2017, LinkedIn had secured 500 million members in 200 countries. Its core function is a professional network that "links" you to other users; it also has a social media platform to post professional updates, but this platform does not have nearly the same relevance or reach as Facebook, Twitter or Instagram. LinkedIn's platform is not primarily used for sharing personal posts (I certainly wouldn't post wedding photos on LinkedIn, while I did on Instagram and Facebook), and it's not a significant place for advertising and selling, but it is an important channel of communication between you and your prospective customers and associates.

LinkedIn's sharing platform is a very different platform to Facebook. It's more formal in many ways, and definitely more upmarket, or at least reflects a higher socioeconomic group. I once heard someone suggest that the average user on Facebook is worth about £1 to the platform. On LinkedIn the average user is worth £10. This is because the average salary of people on LinkedIn is believed to be around £100,000, whereas the average salary of Facebook users is close to £20,000. In other words, LinkedIn users, on average, have more spending power. LinkedIn was started as a professional platform, designed to connect people to prospective clients and employers, while Facebook was started as a way of connecting people socially, to their friends. Because of this, LinkedIn is still generally used more for professional communication whereas Facebook is used more for social connections.

LinkedIn is one of the more expensive platforms to advertise on, but the traffic is definitely more qualified. When you advertise on

LinkedIn, you automatically know you are going to be showing your products to people with a much higher net worth – and thus more spending power – than those on Facebook.

LinkedIn is particularly good for making B2B (business to business) connections; you can search and target people based on a particular job title. So, for example, if I want to raise money for a technology project, I can target VCs (venture capitalists). I would also use LinkedIn to contact a journalist, or to connect with other professionals in my field who may want to collaborate with me and make partnerships. It's a great business support network. But you can't discount LinkedIn for B2C (business to customers), especially if your product is business related. I target my LinkedIn network when I am selling a business course.

Google

Having a Google account is essential because you cannot use Google AdWords unless you have a Google account. Having a Google+ profile will help you rank higher in search results but Google+ has not become a significant platform, comparatively. Although Google has some useful business tools, such as "Google Hangout" for conferencing and "Google Docs" for sharing information, there isn't much Google cross-user interaction. However, because you need to use Google AdWords, you really can't implement a digital marketing strategy without a Google account.

Big Data, Big Business

All these platforms have subtle differences in what they are best for. LinkedIn is good for targeting people based on their professional interests, whereas Facebook and Instagram are better for targeting people based on their *personal* interests. LinkedIn helps me target a specific company name, or people with specific skills or qualifications (because of the information I can gather from their professional profiles). Facebook is better for helping me target people based on their hobbies and their location. Twitter and Instagram are great for targeting people based on their behaviour (like who they are following, what TV shows they watch, where they work out, etc.) For example, as the author of books for entrepreneurs, I can target all people who follow the TV show *Dragons' Den* on Twitter. If you have a product that helps people lose weight, you might look for followers of *The Biggest Loser*. You could do some laser targeting and specifically market to people who tweeted about those shows most often.

Whether you like it or not, every single thing you do online is being recorded. Big Data is a record of every click on Facebook, every tweet, every follow, everything you comment on … every item you buy online. Why do you think your social media accounts are free? Because they are information-gathering tools. Even privatised accounts are monitored. It might feel scary but it's the world we now live in. While this might make *you* feel uncomfortable, you have to think of how it can work to your advantage, for your business. Every piece of information that every business or advertiser could ever want is being recorded. You can't change this fact, so you may as well use it!

The Unparalleled Power of Google and Facebook

By now, you've probably worked out that **Google** and **Facebook** more or less own the world! With Google's parent company owning YouTube, and Facebook owning Instagram (and, since 2014, the increasingly popular messaging and calling application called WhatsApp, which has recently announced the development of a business platform to provide a competitive communications service to businesses) there are few ways in which we communicate in cyberspace that are not through channels owned by Google and Facebook. What does this mean? That you must pay close attention to all the developments these companies are making because, whatever their competitors (who are few and far between) come up with, they have the power to outperform them.

As I've mentioned several times, much of the *specific* information in this book will be out-dated by the time you read it. All I can do is give you an overview of the tools currently available; it's your responsibility to keep up with upgrades and new features, and you must constantly review what is new. If you did some training on running a Facebook campaign a year ago, don't expect what you learned to be entirely relevant today! These platforms, and the tools you can use on them, are constantly evolving. You have to keep up with the changes, and thus keep up with your training. Look at how Facebook Live is constantly being improved, in terms of quality and functionality. Facebook also, not so long ago, introduced a new feature allowing us to "react" to a post, rather than just "like" it, so now we have more scope for communicating our emotions; we can say whether we "love" a post, or show that it makes us sad or angry or shocked. It's hard to remember a time when we were only able to "like" something! This is yet another example of how powerful social media users are. Social media companies respond to what users say they want. Those new Facebook reaction buttons were a *response* to what users said they wanted.

Above all else, simply remember the core message of this chapter, which is: **you must use all the latest tools on the major social media platforms in your digital marketing campaign** so that you can run your campaigns as efficiently and effectively as possible, and you can compete favourably with your competitors.

Branding in the Digital Age

Open a private browsing window (so that your browser doesn't pick up any previous searches) and Google your name and/or business name. This will allow you to see the first thing someone will see if they do a Google search for you and/or your business. Are you happy with what they will see? If not, work hard at changing. Fix your SEO, hire a reputation manager, seek advice from a digital agency… do *whatever it takes* to ensure that the first thing people see when they Google you is the brand message you want to portray.

These days, unless you work actively to maintain the separation, it is very hard to separate you the person from your business brand. In most cases it's advisable *not* to separate you from your brand while you are establishing it. You want to be known for your skills and per-sonality, but you may, one day, want to apply them to a new brand. Furthermore, oftentimes people want to put a face to the business so your image is important. To begin with, you are most important part of your business branding. If part of your business is you, your personality and your expertise, then you, yourself, are a brand. You may be linked to that particular business at this moment in time, but if you sell that business or start a new business, you want to be able to take "brand you" with you.

Anita Roddick became famous for starting The Body Shop, which became a recognised global brand, but as time went on, the entrepreneur became a brand herself, lending her name and the "Anita Roddick" brand to several charitable organisations.

Your online presence *is* your brand. Your social media pages reflect *you* and are part of your branding. You need pages and feeds for both you and your company, *and* potentially for your products. Think carefully about maintaining a good balance between integration and separation between your own brand and the brand of your company. You never know when your company might fold, or not belong to you any more. But you, yourself, will always continue as a businessperson in your own right. Your skills and experience belong to you, not your company, and there is intrinsic value in that.

These days, we are all businesspeople; we all have a personal brand, because we are all digitally depicted by our social media profiles. Nurture your personal brand; grow it and protect it. Use your business to leverage it, but never forget that "brand you" is almost more important than your business brand. In many ways, your personal brand/profile is the most valuable thing you own because no one can replicate it!

Brand You

Many of the most successful brands in the world are closely related to the person who started it. That person's profile and personality is a big part of why the business became successful and thus the company is "branded" by that person's skills and goals. Think about Apple, intrinsically linked to Steve Jobs (almost more so since his death, as people talk about a marked difference between the period when he was alive and now), Virgin and Richard Branson, Disney and Walt Disney, Dyson and James Dyson, Microsoft and Bill Gates, Facebook and Mark Zuckerberg, Chanel and Coco Chanel (and most big designer clothing brands), and many more.

How much do you lend your brand to your business and products? What is your trademark? What is your stamp? What are the images, words and stories that set you apart from the next person? Using your personality within your brand is smart, because it is the one thing you can guarantee will always be unique. No one else is you. Far too many people try to fit in when they should be doing everything to stand out. People are always producing existing products, or having new products copied by other companies, but no one can recreate the real you. There is no other *you* in the world, so use who you are when you brand your business.

Again, think of the Apple brand, it is not only associated with the Apple logo and products, but also with the brains and personality of Steve Jobs. The brand is inextricably linked with his story, and his story is almost a modern legend, so much so that *two* feature films were made about him shortly after he died. People are fascinated about Steve Jobs, the man, and even compare the performances given by both actors who portrayed him (Ashton Kutcher in 2013 and Michael Fassbender in 2015).

You can come up with all kinds of clever concepts for products and attractive logos, but the heart of your branding should start with you. The one thing no one can compete with is *you*. You are the one unique part of your business so use "brand you" in your company's brand.

Building your Brand Awareness

There are several ways in which you can build your profile and brand awareness. To consistently validate and strengthen your brand you should be working towards using all of the following:

1. **Branding by association**

   When people see your brand at the same time as another famous brand or person, they associate it with that brand or person. The fastest way to increase your exposure and raise the profile of your brand is to get leverage (positional advantage) by asking someone with an already high profile to endorse your brand. This is why big companies use celebrities. David Beckham earns a fortune for his endorsements of products such as Sainsbury's, Armani and Gillette. David Beckham is an international icon based on his footballing achievements for England and Manchester United, so when he appears in an advert, people pay more attention to the advert – and thus the product – than if some unknown model or actor was appearing in it. This works on a subliminal level as well as a conscious one. Hiring a celebrity to advertise your product is an extremely effective way of raising awareness of your brand.

2. **Branding by PR**

   PR stands for Public Relations, in other words, your relationship with the public … anywhere the public can see you. This includes your appearance in traditional media (newspapers, magazines, radio, TV, etc.) The best way to get interviews with respected journalists and articles is to hire a publicist with good connections. If you can't afford to hire a publicist, you can write articles and post them on open press distribution channels such as PRWeb and hope they get picked up by media outlets. You can also try to contact the media directly, for example writing to magazine editors and calling radio stations. When you are starting out, you are more likely to have success if you target local media with a local story. Think of ways in which you can attract the interest of local media. For example, if your business is sponsoring a local charity run, or running an educational event in a school, hopefully your local media channels will cover it (as long as you announce it in good time to let them know about it so that they can make the necessary arrangements to cover it). You should also target specialist magazines relevant to your business. For example, I get articles into the *Your Property Network* magazine based on my expertise. Good PR will always shine a positive light on you and affect the way people perceive you. Branding is all about how people perceive you.

3. **Branding by third-party authority**

What people say about you – whether they are right or wrong – will affect how others see you. You cannot always control what people say about you, but wherever and whenever you can, you should. Any positive endorsement is good; whether it is by someone who is famous or not. One person telling another person that they like your products (giving a testimonial) is an essential part of confirming your credibility. Every business needs testimonials, whether they are in writing, recorded as video content or just an audio recording. People going on record to say positive things, about you and your products, is always good for your branding. Get people to be *specific* in their testimonials. You can also use these testimonials to help prospective customers get over any objections. For example, if a potential new customer is saying the product is too expensive, show them a recorded testimonial from someone explaining the value of your product. Ask anyone giving a testimonial to begin by saying, "This is the best product because … " And try to get **industry experts** to give you testimonials. Anyone saying good things about you is helpful, but the best type of "third-party authority" is from industry experts.

If you can get people who are well-known experts in your field to endorse you, that will give you third-party authority as well as branding by association. This is even stronger than branding by association by a celebrity because everyone knows that the main reason the celebrity is endorsing the product is because they are being paid a high (often huge) fee, whereas an expert providing a testimonial is freely supporting you based on the results they've experienced.

4. **Branding by speaking**

Public speaking has become massively important in building awareness for your brand (which is why I teach a course on it). There are many ways in which you can draw attention to your business and promote your brand by speaking in public. You can speak at events, on stages in front of large audiences. You can give interviews. You can even record yourself speaking and upload it to your website, or put a short video of yourself speaking on the major video-sharing platforms (YouTube and Facebook). When you speak, people take in everything about you, the tone of your voice, what you look like (if you speak to them live or record it on video), your enthusiasm and so on. The ability to speak to people gives you the opportunity to educate them about your business, your brand and your products. If you become very successful, you might get invited to speak at other people's events, perhaps to give keynote speeches (although you would normally need a speaking agent for this). If you are invited to be interviewed, for broadcast on TV or an online channel, it's a good idea to get a set of questions first, so that you can prepare. Sometimes you will be asked to provide the questions yourself, although the bigger the show, the less control you get.

5. **Branding by social media**

Finally, of course, we come back to social media. **Your social media feeds are probably the most important branding tools you have.** For all the reasons we discussed in the previous chapter, you *must* ensure you have a presence across all the social media platforms. You have so much scope here to build brand awareness because you can post material – pictures, video, audio – that reflect your brand, that tell people who you are, what you do and what you are selling.

Do you have a Business or a Brand?

Now I want to pick up on a point that I made way back at the beginning of the book when I asked the question "What is a business?" and explained that many people think they have a business when all they have is a brand. Remember I said that if it is just a brand you have, it's not a business yet, but is *could be.*

A fairly new phenomenon that has arisen as a result of the massive growth of social media platforms, the sophistication of online tools for building websites, and the power of viral marketing, is the ability to build a fairly successful brand without even actually having a business to speak of. You can create a website, a fancy logo, professional business cards and cool stickers. All these things help to create a brand, but do not necessarily mean you are a business. Every business has a brand, even if that brand is extremely weak. The name of your business *is* your brand. If you are called "Cars For You" and you are selling second-hand cars, you still have a brand, even if the logo on your shop front is simply written out in black typeface.

However, not every brand is a business.

The definition of a functioning business, as I explained before, is an entity that is trading goods and services. Even if you have a million followers on Twitter and everyone knows your name (and thus your brand), unless you are selling something or exchanging value in some way, you are not a business, you are still only a brand – although in this situation, you could easily turn your brand into a business by monetising your following, something we will come on to discuss in a moment.

The relative ease of creating websites and social media pages these days is a double-edged sword because many people make the mistake of thinking they have a business when they only have a brand. All too quickly you can convince yourself you have a business simply because you have registered a company name, designed a logo and created a following around an idea. That's all fine, great in fact, but you *still* have to create the actual business, you still have to sell something and create revenue, otherwise you only have a brand, not a business.

Even though you can turn a brand into a business, a brand will always be more powerful if it evolves out of a business. My brand – *Wealth Dragons* – actually evolved out of two businesses: mine and that of my business partner, Vincent Wong. We were two guys with property businesses. We came together to hold events teaching people how to create successful property businesses, and Wealth Dragons was born. The more events we did, the more people wanted to buy into who we were and what we did. The brand has gone from strength to strength. Wealth Dragons has been successful, in my opinion, because people like *why* we do what we do. Remember, people don't buy *what* you do, they buy *why* you do it.

Turning a Brand into a Business

I've often been asked the question, "What comes first, the business or the brand?" The answer is, it can be either, because these days you can build a brand first and then turn it into a business.

A whole new world of celebrity has been created in cyberspace. With no barriers to entry, anyone can promote themselves online and build a fan base. Ordinary people are creating followings of millions of fans simply by posting photos and video content, and finding an audience for them. Sometimes, these people become so powerful and such important channels of communications for advertisers that they become known as **social media influencers**. Big brands are becoming aware of the social media influencers out there and have realised that these social media "stars" can help sell their products by endorsing them. Furthermore they will often do it for a fraction of the price that big movie and TV stars would charge, so the companies get much better VFM (value for money). The world of celebrity has shifted dramatically as people have become able to take control of their own brand.

The best thing about using social media influencers to sell your products is that you know you are promoting your product to a completely targeted audience. If I want to sell vegetarian shoes and I put an ad on the TV or radio, a large majority of the people I am paying to advertise to will probably have little or no interest in vegetarian shoes. Whereas if I pay (probably a fraction of the price) for a big vegetarian social media influencer to endorse my product, I am sure to get much higher conversion rates! The more targeted your audience, the better VFM you get from your advertising budget. This can give you even better ROI than using celebrities. If you are asking Taylor Swift to sell a new brand of coffee, no matter how much someone loves Taylor Swift, if they don't like coffee, they are not going to buy the product. Taylor Swift is not (as far as I know) at the heart of the coffee universe! However, if you ask someone who has created an entire following based on a love for coffee to endorse coffee, someone who has positioned themselves as a *coffee expert*, then you know that their followers love coffee.

If you have a business, you can make it a significant part of your marketing plan to identify and approach relevant social media influencers. As your own brand gains traction you can also get creative in terms of exchanging promotional campaigns with people. For example, I know a guy with a million followers on YouTube and I have a million followers on Facebook; I could approach him and suggest I post one of his videos on my Facebook page in exchange for him posting one of my videos on his Twitter feed.

Take a good look at the products and services you are selling and try to match them up to what people are promoting on social media. Then consider whether you could use social media influencers to market your goods.

How to Become a Social Media Influencer

Yes, you too can become a social media influencer! In fact anyone can, it's a complete meritocracy out there. It takes a tremendous amount of work, but if you are focused and follow the right steps, there is absolutely no reason why you can't become one.

If you think you have a personality, or a message or skill, or are an expert in a particular subject, that people might be attracted to, you can build a following and then **monetise your following**. This is what people like Kim Kardashian have done: they have literally turned themselves into a brand and then monetised that brand by lending it to different businesses. They are more or less "famous for being famous". People have been doing this for some time, but now they have an even more powerful way of monetising it. People like the Kardashians can command a huge fee for posting a picture that simply has a product in the background.

If you can be focused and dedicated, it's really not that difficult to become a serious social media influencer. It's hard work, yes, but it's not complicated, it's just about sticking with it and plugging away at it.

With my Facebook following of over one million, I have enough followers to be considered a social media influencer, and I have people approaching me all the time offering me a fee to endorse their products. How did I do it? Honestly, all I have done is post

high-quality, **relevant** content, **consistently** for the past 10 years. People follow me and stay with me because I have not stopped posting interesting content. They like what I post and engage with it. I recently posted a video that got 13,000 shares; the video has been viewed by over a million people in just three months!

You have to post material that people are so excited about they can't wait to share it. How do some big-budget films become so popular while others tank? Well, much of it depends on word of mouth. Any Hollywood studio can more or less guarantee a big opening weekend if they throw enough money (in star value and advertising) at a film, but once word is out on the street, if the film isn't good, people will hear about it on social media and they won't go and see it. The quality has to be consistent. The same goes with social media content. Even if you build a great following by posting good-quality content, if your quality drops off, you'll soon see your engagement drop. It's ruthless out there! Building a solid, sizeable social media following is not rocket science, anyone can do it... but it requires hard work and a lot of discipline. A lot of people don't have the ability to put in what it takes!

Building your Following

Building a social media following takes three massively important things: **time**, **dedication** and **discipline**. Many people think they have these three things, but really they don't. And that is why, even if they get off to an initial good start, they will often end up failing.

If you really want to succeed, though, there is nothing standing in your way. I've been posting content for years and can confirm that the practicalities of posting and getting people engaged have actually never been easier. There are bigger and better channels than ever, people are more engaged than ever, the systems for sharing information are easier to operate than ever... it's *never* been so good! People live and breathe social media; they are obsessed in the same way people became obsessed with TV in the 1970s and 1980s, when advertising budgets really swelled. If you are not taking advantage of the surge in social media interaction and usability, don't complain when you struggle to sell your products!

A couple who work out at my gym have managed to build a massive Instagram following simply by being disciplined and dedicated to it. They take pictures of each other working out and post them to their Instagram feed. Companies have recently started to approach them, offering them money to wear branded workout clothes, or at least place a branded product in the background of a shot.

If you want to become a social media influencer, pick a good topic of interest and talk about it. It's that simple. Talk about your topic *every day*; post **great content** … *every day*. Many people fail to become significant social media influencers because their content is not relevant or interesting, or because they drop the ball and stop posting for a while. Followers can be ruthless, they will quickly move on if you stop engaging with them. It's very much "out of sight, out of mind" … much more so than in real life when, if you go on holiday and don't see someone for a while, they are not going to drop you as a friend. On social media, people have too many choices; they won't wait around for you to start posting again. As I said, it's ruthless out there!

It really is about **discipline** … the discipline to post every day, and keep your content fresh and interesting. You need to make people go "wow". **When you are becoming a social media influencer, your content is your product.** Look at it that way, like everything you post is product. You need to be selling **good product**. It can't be boring. Make people curious; make them want more. Remember, it's not *what* you do it's *how* you do it. Deliver your product in a way that makes people want more!

Going Viral

If you can get a piece of content to go viral, this will give you a massive surge in followers. For a video or image to go viral it has to have that "wow factor"; people have to say "wow" when they see it. It also needs to make you and/or your products (depending on whether the focus of your marketing is on positioning yourself as an expert or on educating people about your products) look amazing. Look at all the features and factors of videos that have recently gone viral. Do your research and try to recreate some of those elements. First and foremost, your content must grab people's attention; additionally it should add value to your brand.

Followers: To Buy or Not To Buy

Getting followers for all your social media profiles is an on-going uphill battle. There was a time when buying followers on Twitter or

Instagram was a totally accepted practice. These days you can tell if someone bought followers. People are far too savvy and will see through a contrived account. If you have 200k followers but very little engagement (i.e. only a handful of likes on every picture), it's obvious you bought your followers. If you bought your followers they are probably people who have nothing in common with you, who are not sharing your interests, and therefore won't engage with you, so it really doesn't help you that much. What *is* acceptable is to build your followers through "follow-for-follow", which is when you follow someone in order to get them to follow you back. Then you will get a qualified audience because you will follow people who follow accounts that are similar to your interests. You are not just looking for followers, you are looking for *engaged* followers, and you will only get those by following people who are likely to be interested in your posts.

Any social media page with a high following can be monetised. Indeed, social media accounts, themselves, have become commodities. I regularly get five-figure offers from people wanting to buy my Facebook page because I've got over a million followers. This is the new **virtual real estate**. You are building a valuable asset in cyberspace, and you can sell that asset. Perhaps we could view this as today's version of selling "lists" that was extremely popular a few years ago (companies would gather names and contact details in a database and then sell those lists to other companies). I actually still get offers for my list. People regularly get in touch with me and offer me thousands of pounds to send out one single email to my list!

YouTube Stars

One of the most powerful ways in which people have capitalised on a social media following is through the YouTube channel. Being a YouTube star or a "**YouTuber**" has become a massively lucrative business. You are effectively a TV channel with a completely targeted audience. If you build a big enough following on YouTube, advertisers will flock to pay you to advertise their product. "YouTuber" has become a legit job title.

The power of YouTube is such that it has launched whole careers. Justin Bieber is a great example of an international superstar whose career was started thanks to the power of social media. He started his career from his bedroom when he was only 13 by posting videos of song covers on YouTube. An influential music industry executive saw his channel and the rest is history.

There are no barriers to entry anymore. It used to be that you needed a record label to give you a deal before your music could be heard. Now, you can self-release music through all the same channels as the record labels. Most people listening to your music on Apple music or Spotify would have no idea whether you have a record deal or have self-released it. Indeed, one of the world's most successful hip hop and R&B artists, Chance the Rapper, who won three Grammy Awards in 2016 including "Best Rap Album" for *Coloring Book*, the first streaming-only album to win a Grammy, created and released all his music with no involvement from a record label.

Having no barriers to entry is another double-edged sword though. It increases opportunity but it also increases competition. You have to do more to stand out. But if you *do* have the talent, you can be seen. And you can create your own celebrity status.

The Florida-based band Boyce Avenue started making and releasing their music videos on YouTube and got an immediate following. To date they have had over 300 million views. They tour regularly and people pay to go and see them live. They used the Internet to build their following and become successful.

YouTuber Alex Day is a British musician who chose to release his songs on his YouTube channel first, before releasing them for sale. He has had three Top 40 hits and, at time of writing, holds the Guinness World Record for highest charting single by an unsigned artist. His single *Forever Yours* reached number four in the UK Singles chart in 2011.

In the same way that musicians can use the Internet to reach potential fans without having to go through a record company, *you* can reach your potential customers without going through traditional channels of advertising and marketing.

The point I want to stress here is that *anyone can make it.*

I was recently approached by Master Wong, a YouTube star who has over a million subscribers to his channel. He is a martial arts expert who speaks in pigeon English with a very strong accent. He's not as polished as some celebrities, but people these days are more interested in seeing authenticity than glitz and glamour. People want reality and full transparency; they want to see someone they can relate to. Always keep this in mind as you are building your business and brand. If you do your research and follow the rules, there's no reason why you can't be a success. If a martial arts expert speaking in pigeon English can do it, so can you. All the tools are out there and available to everyone. **If you want a million followers, you can get a million followers**, you just have to work extremely hard, but no one can stop you. Once you've got a million followers, you can engage with those followers and promote whatever you want to sell to them. It doesn't matter if you are making music or food, teaching photography or martial arts, you need customers. If your potential customers don't know you exist, you cannot sell to them.

You will find there is an appetite for pretty much *anything* on social media. Whatever you're into, whatever your talent, whatever you are selling, virtually whatever you can conceive of … you will find an audience for it somewhere in cyberspace!

Even the financial markets are taking note of the power of social media. Businesses are getting actually valued on their following. Casey Neistat started a YouTube channel in 2010 and began vlogging about various issues. He fast became the "Steven Spielberg of viral videos". In 2016, he sold his company to CNN for $25 million. In the summer of 2017, his YouTube channel had over seven million subscribers. That's on par with the average audience of Britain's Got Talent! What advertiser is not going to pay to advertise on that channel? And, again, the big selling point of a YouTube channel to a business or advertising agency is that it has a completely targeted audience. There's a guarantee that subscribers are interested in the specific topic that the YouTube star promotes. If you're an advertiser and you've got the choice between spending a huge amount of money for a 30-second advert on TV that's going to be seen by a broad audience, or a smaller amount for an advert seen by the same number of people but a specifically targeted audience, where would *you* choose to spend your money?

In the age of social media, and massive competition, targeted viewers are highly valuable.

CHAPTER

10

Cautionary Tales (Adapt or Die!)

As I mentioned earlier, Google and Facebook pretty much control our online lives. But why do you think that is? Maybe it's because they figured out, before any other company did, exactly what Internet users would want. They predicted the future; at least the future needs of Internet users. We don't all use Facebook just because it's got a cool logo and an interesting history, we use it because we *like it* and it serves our needs, because it gives us all the tools we want and need in order to connect with people online.

There are so many success stories of companies that pre-empted the way we would want to consume products and services. Often they have "disrupted" the market. Think about Uber, a company that has totally disrupted the taxi industry. Airbnb has diverted a huge amount of business away from hotels. Adam Sandler has reinvented the movie star model by making films that bypass the studios and movie theatres, and go straight to Netflix as a sole distributor. In March 2017, Netflix announced that Sandler had renewed his exclusive deal with them for a further four movies (following his initial deal to make four movies that he negotiated in 2014). Ricky Gervais has followed suit, stating that he gets more creative control when he makes movies for Netflix rather than the traditional Hollywood studios. This should tell you that there is a massive market for subscription services. These examples have certainly shaped my latest business plans, which include an ambitious online subscription service.

Changes in the way products and services are distributed – the new ways in which you can deliver information or products to your customers – give you far more control. You can even dramatically reduce production costs by keeping everything digital. You can release a book digitally and never print it as a physical book. Similarly you can release a song digitally and never make a CD. Information and education can also be delivered digitally through webinars and e-books. There are more opportunities than ever to make money online, but you *have* to be aware of these changes or you risk being left behind.

For every success story there are plenty of stories about businesses that made the wrong decisions and got left behind. Here are just a few stories of companies that failed because they didn't adapt with the times or predict what consumers would want, in terms of both the products they would want and the ways in which they would want to consume that product.

Blockbuster vs Netflix

Netflix started in 1997 as a rental-by-mail company, allowing customers to order a DVD, watch it and then return it by mail. At the time, this was the very next step in convenience. There was no limit to the rental period and you could keep your DVD as long as you wanted; you would be sent the next DVD from your selected list once you returned the one you had. Then Netflix introduced a subscription service with different levels. So you would pay a set amount per month rather than per DVD. The basic level allowed you to have one DVD at a time and a limited number of rentals per month. The top level allowed you to have three DVDs from your list out at a time and an unlimited number of rentals per month. With so much convenience and choice, compared to the old video store rental model, customers flocked to them.

Until the late 1990s, Blockbuster was the market leader in video and DVD rental, through their global network of stores. But as more and more customers discovered Netflix, where they were won over by the convenience of not having to go to a physical store, and being able to keep their DVDs for as long as they wanted, Blockbuster's sales began to suffer.

With its subscription model, Netflix was perfectly positioned to enter the streaming market and offer unlimited viewing. With its infrastructure in place and ready to enter the twenty-first century as the leader in home entertainment provision, the owners of Netflix offered to sell the company to Blockbuster for $50 million in 2000. But **Blockbuster declined the offer**. This turned out to be a terrible decision because by 2010, just 10 years later, Blockbuster was filing for bankruptcy while Netflix was bringing in revenue of over $2 billion, with 20 million subscribers around the world. By the beginning of 2018, Netflix was worth over $100 billion (market cap).

With rapid technological developments, the way we consume our entertainment has changed dramatically in a very short space of time, and Netflix has been perfectly positioned to service our changing needs. We no longer need a television to watch our entertainment. We don't even need a physical tape or disc; we can download directly from the Internet and even stream live content. New smartphones are so sophisticated, we can even watch in high-definition on our phone screens.

There is obviously no telling whether Blockbuster would have enjoyed the exact same success with Netflix had it acquired the company back in 2000, but there is no denying that the success of Netflix is due to the company's ability to foresee how people would want their entertainment delivered in the future (i.e. streamed online), and Blockbuster's *in*ability to predict this left them unable to compete.

(As an aside: given the increasing power of YouTube and the success of its associated company, Google, Netflix might be wise to keep looking over its shoulder! This applies to any dominant player in technology, because developments happen faster and faster, and you never know when you might be overtaken. Ultimately no one can guarantee that the future they predict will realise so, really, it's important to cover all your bases.)

Barnes & Noble vs Amazon

There has been much debate and discussion over whether the digital delivery of books will ever take over physical book sales. Recent figures show that there has actually been a slowing down in the growth of the digital book market and that physical book sales are strengthening again. People, it seems, still want to own and read physical books. In a similar trend, despite the massive trend in the digitisation of music, vinyl records have really made a comeback and are becoming increasingly popular again.

But *how* people purchase and receive their physical books *has* changed dramatically. People are increasingly choosing to shop online rather than in physical bookshops. Big book chains have started to create online shops, but Amazon has already cornered the market in terms of online shopping. By offering almost anything for sale on its website, specialist stores can't compete with Amazon. If you are on Amazon buying cleaning products, dog food and vitamins, why would you check out and then go to Barnes & Noble (physically or online) if you also want to buy some books? You wouldn't. You would add them to your Amazon shopping cart and then check out, paying for everything in one go.

Amazon gives businesses the opportunity to skip the middleman, or at least use a more reasonably priced middleman. With its "print on demand" feature, Amazon also allows authors and publishers to offer their books at a much lower price, and/or increase their profit margins. It doesn't make business sense to sell through Barnes & Noble or Waterstones any more.

A particularly sore spot for Barnes & Noble is the failure of its e-reader, the *Nook*, to compete with Amazon's *Kindle*. Like Netflix, Amazon pre-empted the way people would consume entertainment, in particular their reading material, and developed a device that could be linked to your Amazon account so that you could effortlessly download books. By the time Barnes & Noble came out with their version, Amazon had cornered the market.

HMV vs iTunes, Spotify, Deezer, etc.

Finally, and briefly, in a similar story to the way digitally streamed film content led to the demise of DVDs, the delivery of digital music seems to have contributed to the sharp decline of the CD industry. By 2015, digital music revenue had overtaken physical CD sales, globally, for the first time. The demise of music stores like HMV, a company that went into administration in 2013, is certainly related to the rise of digital music sales and streaming. HMV went out of business because they didn't adapt to the way consumers wanted to receive their music.

All of these stories relate to the way in which we receive and consume our products. Each year, for example, we see an increase in online sales at peak consumer activity times like Christmas. High street shops are struggling while online retailers are seeing their businesses grow year after year. If you are a business, you can't compete with that trend, you just have to go with it! People shop in an entirely different way from the way they shopped even a few years ago.

You used to be able to interest potential customers in new products by putting them near the regular products that people repeat buy in shops. Now people repeat buy regular products online. If you want to catch their attention, you can't just put your new product beside the toilet rolls in aisle 5, you need to advertise online.

What's the biggest lesson you should learn here? If you're a company providing a product or service, and someone comes along and says, "Hey, I think I've found the next way in which people are going to receive and consume products ... " you should at least listen to them!

Life never stands still, it moves forward exponentially at an ever-increasing rate. The key message here is: **in business, you must adapt or you'll die**. You need to keep looking to the future and stay observant. The more you understand about people's future needs, the greater chance you'll have of creating products that will survive in such fast-moving times.

PART

III

THE FUTURE RULES

11

Predicting Future Trends

You cannot underestimate the speed at which the digital world evolves and new technology replaces the old. You must embrace new tools and functions as they are introduced or you get left behind. One of the ways you can ensure you are able to do that is to **stay ahead of the curve**. If you can get a jump-start on whatever's coming next, *you* will be the one with the advantage over your competitors.

So how do you keep up with the rapidly evolving world of technology?

Out with the Old, in with the New

You can see exponential changes in business wherever you look; even the *speed* at which businesses change is increasing. If you look at the S&P index (Standard & Poor's list of the top 500 US companies based on market capitalisation and other criteria), you can see how fast things are changing these days. Businesses used to last 30, 40, even 50 years on that list. Now the average time a company spends on the list is just 13 years and this will probably soon drop down to 10 years. This shows you exactly how tough the competition is. And investors are ruthless. If you were once in the S&P 500 but you drop out of the list, you're as good as finished; no one is interested in an *ex*-S&P 500 company.

But competition is healthy and these fast fluctuations show that barriers to entry are always being lowered, that new companies are constantly coming up through the ranks and making it into the list. It means that the world today is more of a meritocracy, which means that there is more opportunity for everyone. All businesses have to stay on their toes, no one can afford to sit back and roll along, just seeing what happens!

Every 10–15 years the "latest" technological platforms get replaced. Google, Facebook and Instagram have more or less replaced similar platforms that were prevalent 15 years ago, such as Yahoo!, Friends Reunited and AOL. It is not inconceivable to imagine that there are new platforms, in development now, that will eventually replace everything that we all take for granted now. There is actually a logical reason for this that is related to the natural progression of any ambitious business. As organisations get bigger, they become slower at evolving. This is because the expectations of a public company are different from those of a private company. For example, Facebook was once a small private company that could do anything it wanted. It was niche; it was cool; it was adventurous. Since its IPO in 2012, Facebook has had to answer to shareholders. The company is a huge business now and they can't take too many risks; they are motivated by profit. They might be able to upgrade a few features here and there, but in general they have to play it safe.

What this means in the wider context is that all the features that Facebook can no longer explore are probably being developed by another business somewhere. If you want to stay ahead of the curve, **find that business and keep up to date with its progress!** Even if you can't pinpoint a specific company, one thing is certain, there are probably many companies researching how AI (artificial intelligence) is going to affect the way we operate and engage with each other.

The AI Revolution

While you are reading this and thinking about your social media pages – worrying about which picture to post or which article to share – somewhere else in the world, robots are designing aircraft engines better than humans can!

AI is not science fiction, it is real and it is developing fast. If you really want to stay ahead of the curve, you should be researching AI and learning everything you can about the latest developments.

Quite simply, AI is going to be the next big wave that changes the world. Microsoft, Apple and Facebook already use AI to "help" users. The billionaire entrepreneur, Elon Musk is genuinely concerned about the speed at which AI is being developed and believes it is the biggest threat to the human race. Whether or not AI is a good or bad thing for humanity, one thing is certain... it will disrupt a lot of businesses. You need to be aware, if you are trying to develop a business, whether there is a chance that your products and services could soon be made extinct by AI developments. In your communications, you need to be aware of everything that is being tested now, because it will become commonplace in a blink of an eye. Technological developments move at an exponential speed. Regardless of what will happen in the long term, what does a future controlled by AI look like in the short term? AI is the next big wave in business development because it can make better and faster decisions for business, so you cannot afford to ignore it.

AI is by no means a new concept; it's been around for many years and it is being taken very seriously. As I loosely referred to above, Boeing have been investing massively in AI because it is able to design aircraft parts better than human beings can. AI will provide the optimum design faster than human beings will.

Most of us were introduced to AI through science fiction movies, and that's just what we thought of it as: science *fiction*. But who remembers science fiction movies showing us self-drive cars? A concept that seemed, not so long ago, the stuff of science fiction, is now upon us. Autonomous (self-drive) cars are now being tested and will probably be amongst us before we know it. As of March 2018, Apple was testing 45 autonomous cars.

Any minute now, the AI revolution will be very real and we will be in the middle of it before we know it.

Think Laterally

Big businesses are investing in AI, aware that if they invest now, and achieve a certain level of intelligence, they could make a quantum leap ahead of the curve. Just because you have a small business (although I prefer not to refer to businesses as "big" and "small", because any "small business" can grow into a "big business") and may not have millions of pounds to invest in AI technology, you don't have to get left behind. You *can* do your research and stay informed, and we have never lived in a time where information is so easily obtained. Most importantly, if you think laterally, you can figure out ways in which you could capitalise on the implications of such new technological developments.

For example, if your research tells you that 200 million driverless cars will be on our roads by 2020, what are the implications of that for other businesses? Well, one business that will be changing dramatically will be the car insurance business. With cars being driven automatically, the accident rate will be lower, so car insurance will be much cheaper. If this prediction is true then the car insurance industry will be massively affected. How could you take advantage of that?

Think laterally. How can you ride the wave of technological developments? If you can think of what the *implications* of technological advancements might be, you should be able to make money by creating the products and services that people will need.

Here's another example. Since the introduction of the Sony Walkman, which was eclipsed by the iPod, which has now been incorporated into the smartphone, people have been using headphones more and more regularly. This is having an effect on ear health. People are developing ear problems and hearing problems as a result of overusing headphones. Put your money into technology that helps with ear and hearing issues, and you are probably onto a winner.

Who Wants to Live Forever?

AI has massive and far-reaching implications that we should all take time to think about. There is a widely held belief that AI is going to achieve consciousness, and will start fighting for itself, within our lifetime. That is why people like Elon Musk are so afraid of it. The American futurist Ray Kurzweil has predicted that machines will attain full legal status equal to humans by 2099. He's also predicted some baby boomers (i.e. people born in the post-World War II years) will still be alive at that time, in other words that there will be people living who are 140–150 years old. He has suggested that, if you can stay alive until the year 2045, you have a good chance of living forever. Whether you'd want to or not is another matter! Kurzweil has an 86% success rate with his predictions, so these predictions are worth taking note of. Look him up and read all his predictions for yourself; they are fascinating.

Living forever may sound like the stuff of science fiction, but when you consider some of the latest advancements in the medical sector, you can really see how the notion of staying alive forever could become a reality. We are fast approaching a time when we are going to be able to cure ourselves using our own stem cells. There have been extensive studies into curing heart disease using stem cells harvested from patients' own bodies. Stem cell therapy has already been used in changing hair and skin colour, preventing greying and helping people with conditions like vitiligo.

Who's the Expert Now?

The idea of our bodies lasting forever might be a difficult concept to buy into, but what about the notion of our brains existing independently of our bodies? This is a concept that has been around for a while, in fiction and in actual medical research. So what is a person? Are they their body or are they their brain? When someone is on "life support" but not brain dead, we consider them to be "more alive" than when there is no brain activity, so what exactly is "life" anyway? That's a big existential question!

Within the next 50 years or so, there's a chance that our brains may become software-based. In other words, we will be able to copy our brains and pass them on to someone or something else. Fancy living inside a robot? This also means we can be anything: a doctor, a musician, an astronaut. That scene in the film *The Matrix* where Neo downloads the helicopter pilot programme into his brain suddenly doesn't seem to be so far-fetched now. What will this mean in practice? Well, for a start, the differences between people would not be so pronounced. But when we can all be anything we want, who's going to be the expert when anyone can be the expert?

If we can all be anything we want then how can we differentiate between people in terms of their suitability and qualifications to do a job? Furthermore, one of the problems with AI is that, if machines replace us by doing our jobs more efficiently, then more and more people will become redundant. This is why some countries are suggesting rolling out a **universal basic income**. In 2017, Finland gave a universal basic income to 2,000 citizens as a test project. Participants have reported lower levels of stress and greater incentive to look for work and explore business opportunities. So, far from being gift-wrapped communism, as some critics have called it, it seems that the scheme could be beneficial to human development.

Continuing with the theme of copying your brain as software, let's get even more imaginative and suggest that, as virtual reality (VR) becomes increasingly advanced, it will be harder to tell the difference between virtual reality and what we call are *actual* reality. And, referring back to the core concept of the movie *The Matrix*, how can you be certain that you are not already currently living in a virtual reality world?

But returning to what we are going to, for the time being, accept as our *real world*, there will definitely be changes that occur as menial jobs are taken over by computers. What will you do? What can you do that a computer can't do? The real edge over other human beings will be **original thought**. Unless and until AI *does* take over the world, someone has to drive technology forward and those who understand the development of technology will have a slight edge over others. In other words, as a business owner who needs to communicate with customers, you must keep up with technological advancements. If you can't embrace the technological changes in the world, especially the rapid **digitization of communication**, then you will fast be left behind.

Which Future?

Obviously every single entrepreneur out there is trying to be a fortune-teller. If you're an entrepreneur and you're not desperate to predict the future, you're not being very ambitious. This is why entrepreneurship is no picnic; it's unpredictable, it's competitive and it's risky. The rewards are huge, but there are no huge rewards without huge risks and hard work. Entrepreneurs are not jumping on the latest bandwagon... they are trying to **reinvent the wheel**.

No one can predict, with absolute certainty, the future... but people still try. And everyone has their own personal vision of what the future holds. If there are a million entrepreneurs out there, that's a million different visions of the future. But you must remember this: there **is only one future**. So only one of those entrepreneurs is going to get it right! It's like playing the "prediction lottery".

All I am absolutely certain of is that there is no certainty in life. Ultimately, you have to accept that you cannot 100% guarantee your success in anything. You can work hard, you can stay **curious**, you can stay **involved** in the latest trends and you can stay **informed**, to give yourself the best chance, but you can't *guarantee* anything. You can only do your best.

A Business on Any Scale

There is no scale of business that should be deemed "too big" or "too small" for an entrepreneur. If you are building a business, it could be on any scale. It could be a small-scale business in a tiny niche market, or it could be as huge as space exploration. Elon Musk might be one of the most successful businessmen in the world, but he is still an entrepreneur. He is currently working towards the privatisation of space exploration. He is building space shuttles. This is not a business that needs to *advertise* on Facebook at this point in time, but he is still creating content to publicise his SpaceX brand. The latest videos show incredible simulated footage of how people would be able, in the near future, using his spacecraft, to travel from New York to Shanghai in 39 minutes. Find it and watch it; it looks incredible and will revolutionise our lives when it happens, in the same way that commercial air travel was a complete game changer.

You don't need to be a rocket scientist to build a million-dollar business with all the tools that are available to you. As I've said before, there are fewer and fewer barriers to entry. If you really want to build a million-dollar business, you can. But a *billion*-dollar business is whole different ball game. A billion-dollar business is going to affect a huge number of people. No one is building a $1 billion+ business that is not going to have a profound effect on the lives of people throughout the world. Again, think of the airline business. It revolutionised the world because it allowed ordinary people to travel the world quickly. The first commercial airline flight was in 1914, just over 100 years ago. Where will we be at the start of the twenty-second century? This is what entrepreneurs like Elon Musk are constantly thinking about. They are thinking on a scale of 50, 100, even 200 years from now, they are thinking about how the businesses they are building now will affect our lives far, far into the future. Although it might sound like a sci-fi movie right now, maybe we *do* need to colonise Mars as a safe haven from AI?

These far-thinking entrepreneurs are really doing us all a service. Elon Musk didn't need to be so ambitious for the future of the human race, he could have just built software to sell and made himself a lot of money, but he's chosen projects that move humanity forward on a far-reaching scale. And if he does crack commercial space travel in his lifetime, he will make a *huge* amount of money!

Disrupting the Market

A big buzzword in recent times has been **disruption**. Increasingly it seems as though the entrepreneurial goal for the twenty-first century is to be a successful **disruptor**, in other words to find a new way to "disrupt the market", i.e. find a novel way of providing a product or service that heavily challenges an established market. Earlier in the book I mentioned two of the biggest market disruptors in modern times: **Uber**, who disrupted the cab market with an original business model, and **Airbnb**, who did the same to the hotel market. If you can find a way of successfully disrupting a huge market, your business could explode.

You don't always have to reinvent the wheel; sometimes it's about identifying a successful business model or tool and *applying* it to a new market. Grindr was a highly successful location-based dating app for the gay community. Tinder simply took the features of Grindr and created an app that targeted the heterosexual market. They literally stole the idea and repackaged it. Much like Instagram stole all of Snapchat's core features and repackaged them.

If you can identify an existing successful service and then apply it to a new industry or market, you could have a very successful business! But, as ever, keep it about **what people want and need**.

People Want More Engagement

When it comes to finding out **what people want and need**, it seems, in the first instance, very obvious, judging by the way people behave on social media, that they want **more engagement**.

The latest trend to hit the marketing world is **experiential marketing**, where people are offered the opportunity to learn about a new product not just by reading or hearing about it, but by *experiencing* it. And one of the most exciting technological developments of recent times, something that really complements this trend, is **augmented reality**. I believe that augmented reality (AR) is going to be a hugely popular and effective way of reaching our customers in the future. People want a heightened experience. Think how big the *Pokémon Go* craze became in 2016. That app was powered by AR. Players of the game were transfixed by the idea of being able to see something through the camera on their phone that wasn't really there.

With experiential marketing and AR, you can introduce potential customers to a product in ways they have not experienced before, which could really set you apart from your competition. This is an example of a trend you should research, in order to work out how it might benefit your marketing efforts.

The Power of Algorithms

Algorithms are programmes that read your online activity and curate information from your social media feeds. They are incredibly useful tools for businesses, allowing you to tailor your marketing endeavours and target specific groups, but they are also polarising the world. People are watching television less and less, and relying on their social media feeds that are tailored to their interests and opinions, so they are not receiving much bipartisan information. If you are only receiving news stories that reflect your interests and opinions, how are you getting a balanced view of the world? And how do you know the news you are reading is the truth? "Fake news" has been a hot topic since the beginning of 2017. Algorithms make it possible for the people who know how to use them to drop subtle – and sometimes subliminal – messages into your news feeds. And it now seems like this process may have been used to manipulate elections on both sides of the Atlantic. These tailored messages feel so personalised that you feel they are speaking directly to *you*, so they are very powerful. When you use social media to put your message across, you are in possession of a very powerful tool.

If you want to stay ahead of the curve and predict what people will want and need in the future, you should have a very clear understanding of what they want and need *now*. Algorithms are extremely useful for helping you do that.

Beyond the Digital Age

Finally, when it comes to predicting future trends, think on this. Trends are often cyclical. After the explosion of digital communication, is it possible that society might start to crave human-based connections again? Like vinyl records making a comeback despite the instant availability of digitised music? Think along these lines and see how it inspires you. Keep asking "What do people *need?*" and you might come up with the next big thing to disrupt the biggest market of all … the market that is digital communication!

12

Don't Become a Human Bot!

In the final chapter of this section, at the risk of sounding like I'm contradicting everything I've said before, I want to encourage you to **get off the computer and put down the phone**!

Yes, I have endlessly stressed the importance of being digitally connected in order to grow your business, but now let's talk about the importance of getting *out* of cyberspace and *off* social media to allow yourself to grow as a human being. Because that is what you are: a human being. Don't become a **human bot**!

A "bot" (short for robot) is a software application that runs automated tasks, collecting data and sweeping Internet sites for specific information. When we are aware of the vastness of cyberspace, it is all too easy to get stuck in the role of a bot, never stopping until we absorb all available information – definitely an impossible task!

As much as the Internet is an essential marketplace for you and your business, you mustn't get so sucked in that you forget how to connect in real life. You need to down tools and live in the real world sometimes. Stay connected to friends, family and your social group. Network with professional groups at events. Get out there and get inspired. It's not just essential for your health (your brain, your eyes, your nervous system) but you will take the knowledge you acquire back to your digital world, and it will enhance it.

We all know that social media platforms can be extremely addictive. Social media and phone addiction is a real thing. People are increasingly aware of it and there is a new trend of **digital detoxing** where people take an extended break, a digital retreat, from using all digital devices. Studies have shown that we, as human beings, need time away from electronics to connect in a human way, on a human level, with other human beings. Too much screen time can cause all kinds of problems, from insomnia to narcissism. There are hotels now, where you can check in all your devices at the front desk – talk about creating a solution to a problem people have! My wife and I have dates where we leave our phones at home so that we can't be tempted to look at them while we're at dinner. Otherwise, you can't help yourself. I know people who can't even go to the toilet without taking their phone! We all know how much nicer it is to spend time with someone who is not using their phone. You actually talk to each other and become more engaged in your conversation.

Granted, it's not easy to put down your phone. One of the problems we face is that we are now part of a global community and the world never shuts down. There is no such thing as an evening or weekend when it's Monday morning or Friday afternoon somewhere. No one ever leaves work anymore. We answer emails in the gym, in the movie theatre, even while walking. Our businesses are open 24/7 because people expect a very short response time. It used to be that when you left the office, you left the office … not these days.

It is very tempting to stay glued to your social media, especially when you are building a new business. There's always another person to follow or another article to share, but at the end of the day you still have to get out into the real world. Finding out what is happening to people in their real lives is also an essential part of growing your business. You need to be having real conversations. There really is no substitute for a real, live conversation, face to face with someone, when you are trying to find out what people want and need.

Having said that, putting a screen between you and someone can also have interesting results. Depending on the topic and the person, when you put a screen between them and you, it may give them the chance to be more honest or more dishonest, depending on what their agenda is. You can see this phenomenon very clearly with online dating. People pretend to be what they are not, or they are more courageous in stating what they are looking for, when they can hide behind the anonymity of a dating profile. Regardless, you will usually find that meeting someone online and meeting someone offline are two totally different experiences. What this proves, for better or worse, is that our connections with each other change when there is a screen in the way. So you must make sure that you are interacting and making connections with people both on *and* off the screen.

The lines are very blurred, of course. As a speaker and educator myself, I interact on a daily basis with people in all kinds of ways, both in person and online. I could be messaging with someone on a Facebook thread, then having lunch with someone in a restaurant, and later having a videoconference that is one-on-one, and then finishing up with a webinar streamed to many people. The next day I could spend the whole day at an event speaking to thousands of people. A live event is still a very thrilling experience and you can't really get the same effect with recorded content. It's like the difference between going to see a musician live and listening to their recorded material. I recently went to a Celine Dion concert in Las Vegas. I listen to her music endlessly on CDs, but nothing compares to the experience of seeing her live.

There are various pros and cons of communicating with people online and offline. You definitely have a better chance of capturing someone's full attention when you speak to them offline. Yes, you can send them an email, but you have no idea whether or not they will ever open it. When you speak to them in person, they *have* to listen to you. And you can command their full attention. When they are reading about you or your product online, you are competing with the myriad other things they are doing. At any one time we can all be distracted by countless things going on around us.

If someone comes to listen to you speak in the flesh, you know you know that they are committed to listening to you, that they are more serious. They have invested time in listening to you without distraction. A real music fan will not just buy their favourite musician's CD; they will buy the CD *and* go to the concert. They are fully committed.

When people are communicating with you in the flesh, or on the screen, they know it is you. When they read messages that come from your account, they know it could be anyone writing those messages. There is an authenticity in the flesh that can never be replicated online.

That's not to say that technology isn't always trying to help us recreate this human experience. Think of how emojis have become so popular. This is because they compensate for how, when you are reading a text message, you can't see the expression on someone's face. In real life, we use expressions to determine whether someone is joking or is particularly sad. The exact same sentence said with a smile can come across as having a completely different meaning when said with an angry expression. Sometimes we *need* to read someone's facial expressions to tell whether they are really upset or are joking. Emojis help us communicate our true feelings to the recipient of the message when they can't see our face. Emojis were developed out of *necessity*; online communication is so easily misinterpreted, and emojis help our understanding of the typed message. This is why they are so popular.

Businesses are becoming increasingly cognisant of the fact that people need human experiences. I mentioned experiential marketing in the last chapter, a fast-growing trend where instead of simply *telling* people what products and services are on offer, companies will invite potential customers to *experience* them. Furthermore, they will often invite a *group* of people to come together, so that they can *share* the experience with other human beings. This shows us that the human experience still holds as much, if not more, importance than the digital one.

Remember that the point of creating passive income streams from a business that sells products and services is to buy back your time, to allow you to put down your phone or device and interact with people on a human level. Don't forget to *allow* that income stream to be passive. You must stop obsessing about your business at some point.

Embrace all the technology that exists, but never forget you are a *human being* first and foremost. **You must find the balance between living in the real world and living in cyberspace.**

PART IV

THEIR RULES (CASE STUDIES)

13

Case Studies

The nature of what I do – holding huge motivational events on an international scale, and maintaining an extensive online profile – means that I get many people approaching me asking me to mentor them. I will consider mentoring anyone, but I only have a finite amount of time so it's important I make careful choices. I am very fortunate to have been able to mentor some incredibly motivated and passionate people, and I'm excited to be able to share some of my favourite success stories with you.

My skill is helping people to grow their businesses and encouraging them to seek financial empowerment. Often people don't understand **business and entrepreneurship** or the opportunities that are available to them these days until I enlighten them. People don't generally come to me looking to start a business; they come to me looking to change their lives and I show them how starting a business can help them do that. I create a bridge between them *wanting* to start a new life and them actually *doing* it. I facilitate that journey and show them the way.

I can only work with people who have decided to put the work in, who are ready to start immediately. They have to be committed, feel more than simply a desire to do something; they have to be ready to go for it. I always say there is a difference between an entrepreneur and a *want*repreneur (see Figure 13.1). An entrepreneur has an idea and a month later has a business. A wantrepreneur has an idea and a month later *still* only has an idea.

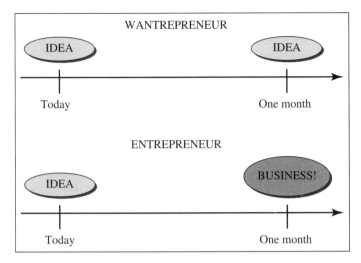

Figure 13.1   The Difference Between an Entrepreneur and a WANTrepreneur

Paying it Forward

My entire business focus is about helping people, about giving them tried and tested techniques that I have discovered myself, that will help them grow their businesses. In turn, they must want to help others. I need to know that my students want to "pay it forward". I can only help people who *genuinely* want to help others. I often come across people who *say* they want to help others, but I can quickly tell whether they are genuine or not. It's easy to say you want to help others when really the motivation is 100% self-interest. I know that I have a genuine mission to help people, so I can identify people who feel the same and set them apart from those who are just paying lip service to the concept of "paying it forward".

When someone asks me to mentor them, the first thing I ask them is why they want me, specifically, to be their mentor. I always listen closely to their answer. If at any point they mention their key motivation is to get rich quickly, or if they start grilling me about what guarantees I can give them, or asking me whether they will earn a certain amount of money in a specific timeframe, I know I can't mentor them, because I know their key motivation is not to help people, it's to make money.

Money should always be the *by-product* of doing what you love and sharing what you know out of a genuine desire to help people, not the main motivator. If prospective students ask me questions like, "How much time do I need to put into this?", or if I detect that someone has too much negativity, I know my coaching will not be right for that individual; we won't be on the same page.

I have to *want* to mentor someone. I feel motivated to help someone when I see that they are very serious about being successful – that they really *want* success. They must also be coachable. I need to know they will listen to me and not be defensive and question me all the time, which I've come across in the past. If they want to talk more than I talk, it's not going to work; they have to be willing to implement my advice *fast* and without asking too many questions. They must trust me. And finally, they must be in the right frame of mind. I have to see that they have the right attitude, that they have a serious desire to help other people. Again, it is this final point that is the most important to me. I believe that at the heart of every successful business is a genuine desire to help people, to serve people, to solve their problems. You have to want to do this to have a good chance of being successful. I believe that, if you can give someone something that improves their life, either by helping them to solve a problem or giving them entertainment to enrich their life ... then you have a product. The only people I want to mentor are those who have a product that will first and foremost help other people, that will make money as a by-product not as a primary goal in itself.

Here are the stories of some of the people (names changed for publication) I have helped.

Christina: Cypriot-based Events Organiser

Christina had been running an events business in Cyprus. She held conferences for entrepreneurs with guest speakers and workshops. We met after I went to hear a mutual friend speak at one of her events. When I attended the event, I happened to notice that she wasn't setting up her room optimally. She had an aisle down the middle of the room. I know, from experience, that if you set up the chairs in your room with an aisle down the middle, you lose energy from the speaker on stage. I pointed this out and she asked me for further advice.

In our first conversation, I asked Christina what her biggest challenge was. She said that the events were going very well but that she simply didn't know how to market them to more people. She was struggling to get her name out there. When I asked her what her goal was she said she wanted to become the biggest promoter of the type of events she organised in Cyprus. I taught her how to run Facebook ads and create videos to help her achieve that goal.

Within 18 months, Christina achieved her goal. She became very well known in her industry and she runs some of the biggest events in Cyprus. As a result, she was approached by Arianna Huffington and now one of Christina's courses is on Thrive, the online learning platform that spun out of Arianna's best-selling book.

Christina's background was similar to that of many people in Cyprus. She was one of the victims of the Cypriot government's bank raid, when the government in Cyprus took savings from people's bank accounts to pay their debts. She woke up one morning to find that her savings had gone. Now she has bounced back by getting her revenue up to six figures in a very short space of time.

As I explained, I choose who I work with carefully. I want to know that they are going to put the work in. I don't want to waste anyone's time and I don't want my time to be wasted. I knew Christina was 100% committed to her business. I also liked the fact that she was determined to *help* people. So many people were severely affected by the Cypriot bank raid, people's lives were ruined and they had to rebuild quickly. Christina helped many people in Cyprus to do exactly that. From the moment I met her, she spoke passionately about the people she wanted to help, always calling them "my people". I really liked that. She would often say, "I never want my people to face such a crisis again." Christina's mission is to teach people how to become successful in their own independent right so that they are never in a position of financial ruin again. I knew her mission to help people was genuine, which is why I chose to mentor her.

I like to take on clients who have powerful stories. Christina's story is certainly very powerful!

Lin: "East Meets West" Business Connections

Lin contacted me after she saw me speak at a big event where I had appeared alongside Bill Clinton. She sent me a message through LinkedIn, saying that she felt we had some common business interests. Lin explained that her business involved connecting Chinese investors with Western businesses. She felt I would get the "East Meets

West" theme that was at the heart of her business and a big part of her brand.

Lin invited me to come and speak at one of her events in central London, and after the event, which was a huge success, we spent some time talking about her business and how I could help her. She asked me to mentor her and, once I saw how committed Lin was to making her business work through helping people make good business connections, I was happy to do so.

What immediately struck me about Lin was that, although she was extremely charismatic and likeable, she wasn't confident, but I really felt there was something special about her, something very strong and genuine, and I was sure I could help her confidence grow. When I asked Lin about her goals, she told me that she wanted to work with high-calibre people and HNW (high net worth) individuals. The irony was that she felt unable to command a high fee for what she was doing. It wasn't until I learned all about her background that I understood why.

Lin was originally from Taiwan and when she had arrived in the UK she was barely able to speak English. In a few short years, Lin's English had improved dramatically and she was able to communicate perfectly well. However, she still carried the humility of someone who once spoke English badly, and her self-worth reflected that. She simply didn't believe in herself. I could see that the language barrier was still holding her back and I was determined to work with her on that.

I also discovered that Lin was from an extremely successful family in Taiwan. Her family had been completely opposed to her move to the UK and had put a huge amount of pressure on her to stay in Taiwan, and were always urging her to move back. I understood this pressure because I know how influential families can be in Chinese culture. It is very much frowned upon to go against your family's wishes or expectations. You are expected to stay in your home town and work in your family business, not fly off halfway around the world to do your own thing. This was another thing I could give her strong advice and encouragement about. She'd encountered a lot of negativity from her family and other people. They would say to her, "You're an Asian woman, you'll never make it." I knew what it felt like to be discouraged and I was determined to help her to prove them wrong, just as I had proved so many people wrong.

In the few years I've been working with Lin, she's transformed. She's come to understand the benefits of having multiple streams of income, and she consistently posts videos to social media to promote her business. Her events have gone from strength to strength. She runs many different types of events for different types of investors, and has even started to run events for property investors in London, connecting buyers and sellers. She has many Hong Kong investors amongst her clients and helps some of them get investment visas for the UK. Lin's business has become so successful and popular she has even started to connect with celebrity clients. She was recently interviewed on television, by a Chinese news station.

Lin's success is inspirational and I'm proud to have worked with her.

Andrew: Scaling Up a Security Business

Andrew approached me after hearing me speak at a wealth creation conference. He explained that he had a security business, involved in the selling and installation of alarms for properties. He was frustrated with how his business was going; he wasn't getting enough sales. I soon discovered that his problem was all to do with scaling and systemisation; he was spending far too much time managing the business himself, so the first thing I did was to suggest some online software he could use to systemise his business, which freed up a lot of his time.

Another problem Andrew had was that 80% of his business came from a small number of big contracts. If any of those big contracts ever pulled out, he would stand to lose a significant chunk of his business. He needed lots more customers with smaller contracts in order to spread the risk. He needed to generate some organic growth but he didn't have any sales people dedicated to generating new business. I encouraged him to hire some people to generate new sales as soon as possible, which he did.

Finally, I looked at how Andrew could scale his business. The main issue was that all his business was focused in one geographical area: Blackburn. I suggested that Andrew could form some strategic alliances in order to expand all over the country. We decided to start by approaching engineers. I was sure that, if Andrew could make a strategic alliance with engineers who were being hired to fit alarms for people, he could incentivise them to sell *his* alarms. We tested the process using the existing engineers he did business with in Blackburn by asking them to try and sell some products directly to customers.

Previously, the process went like this: when a potential customer made an enquiry about having an alarm fitted, an engineer would visit them, write down all the information and then bring all the information back to the office. Back at the office, a sales person would call the customer and try to make a sale. The new system allowed the engineers to carry the product and sell it themselves, directly to the customer, for a commission. We found that they were more likely to a make a sale in this way.

By turning his engineers into "on the ground" sales people, Andrew transformed his business. Once we had tested and honed the process using local engineers, Andrew was able to scale up. He was soon doing business throughout the country because he could send his alarms to engineers anywhere. We used Google AdWords and referral marketing to advertise for engineers. Very soon, Andrew had engineers contacting him from all over the country. Andrew built up a relationship with these engineers and they became his core sales force; they now generate sales, working on commission. We used the Internet for two purposes: firstly to recruit suitable engineers and secondly to get customer leads. It worked particularly well when we could match up engineers to customers. If we got a potential customer contacting us from Leeds, we'd find an engineer in Leeds, put the two of them in touch, and the engineer would make an appointment to go and see the potential customer and hopefully sell them one of Andrew's alarms and fit it for them. Suddenly the business was not location-specific, it was nationwide.

Andrew had been running this business for 35 years before he met me. He was amazed by the results. By changing one simple part of the process, allowing the engineers to become the salesmen, his business was transformed. His business is now a fully automated, nationwide online business.

Recently, Andrew spent two months travelling around Mexico. He was able to do this because he has complete financial freedom! I often tell his story to inspire other business owners.

Janet: From Retail Assistant to Personal Branding Consultant

When Janet first came to one of my events, she was working in retail – as a shop assistant at Chanel – and living on a modest salary. She was passionate about fashion but was frustrated by working for someone else and wanted my help to start her own business. What Janet was especially passionate about was helping people make good fashion choices. The best part of working in retail, for her, was giving people advice when they came into the shop. She wanted to do that more often. She basically wanted to be a stylist. I could see that what motivated her was *helping people* and I was impressed with her passion and determination, so I agreed to work with her.

I soon realised that, like Lin, Janet suffered from a lack of confidence and self-worth; she was shy and found it difficult to approach people. She came to one of my intensive programmes and I helped her get out of her comfort zone and build some confidence deep down inside. I encouraged her to see that, in order to be a consultant to others and help them gain confidence from the way they dressed, *she* needed to come across as more confident herself. She always *looked* immaculate but was hesitant when communicating with people. She was determined to work hard to change this.

Janet gained an enormous amount of confidence through working closely with me. She learned how to speak confidently on stage and how to sell her consultancy service with conviction. I showed her how to use social media to find her audience and connect with it.

The consultancy business that Janet started is now thriving. She has gone beyond basic fashion advice and styling, and now helps people with their personal branding, revamping their whole image with clothes, make-up, hair and shoes, as a package. She puts on branding events in upmarket hotels, and is an international speaker, now having been invited to speak at events around the world. She also does regular Facebook Live events.

I believe that one of the keys factors underpinning Janet's success is that she always shares her own story. Whenever she speaks to people, one to one or at an event, she talks candidly about how under-confident she once was, and explains how she turned her life around. People are always inspired by Janet's story and it helps motivate them on their own journey of personal development.

It's been a pleasure watching Janet's growth, as a person and a business owner.

Kay: Malaysian Boutique Hotel Business

I met Kay at a conference about property investing in Malaysia. She asked me to help her with her boutique hotel business, which involved running a hotel with themed rooms. It was doing fairly well but she wanted to take it to the next level. I loved the nature of Kay's business, and could imagine how much enjoyment her guests got from her unique rooms, so I was happy to help her.

Each of Kay's rooms has a novelty theme. For example, she has a Michael Jackson room and a Hello Kitty room. When I met her she was also in the process of making a Harry Potter room and a Frozen room. I could see she had some great USPs (unique selling points), she just needed to harness the power of social media so that people would find her.

I worked closely with Kay on her branding and social media campaigns. One of her problems is that her hotel is not actually in Kuala Lumpur (the capital of Malaysia), it is about an hour outside of the capital, so she really needed to sell the attraction of the rooms themselves, as she can't really compete in terms of location. When I met her, Kay's occupancy rate, at just over 50%, was not great. The other major problem she had was that she was paying out a lot of money to places like Expedia, sites that got people to stay in her hotel, but took a big percentage of the fee (around 25%). I felt she was paying too much money out to these companies, while at the same time was not getting her occupancy rate up.

Kay needed to address all these issues. My goal was to help her get more exposure herself so that she didn't have to rely on other companies for her business. She needed more personal leads; the answer was obviously social media.

Using social media was great because we could use geo-targeting. Most of Kay's business was coming from Singapore, Thailand, Japan and Malaysia, so we ran adverts to people in those areas as well as fans of the subjects of her room themes. Social media enabled us to get pictures of the rooms straight out to the best potential customers. Adverts featuring pictures of the Michael Jackson room were sent to Michael Jackson fans; adverts featuring the Hello Kitty room were sent to Hello Kitty fans, etc.

We also used Facebook to continue to market to all her existing clients who had stayed with her previously. She had their emails so we uploaded these into Facebook and created an advert to be sent out to all those users. We were able to target most of the people who had ever stayed with her. I explained to her that if she had 1,000 clients who regularly stayed once a year, and we could get them to stay twice a year, then we would have doubled her business.

The results were outstanding. Her occupancy rate went up to 87% and sometimes hit 90%. A few months after I started working with her, she took over 130 bookings by herself (compared to the same period the year before when she had 40). I also helped Kay use Google AdWords more efficiently to advertise her hotel. It had been costing her a fortune to get onto the first page of search results. I tweaked the way she organised her ads by changing the order of her key terms and also found some alternative key terms that cost less money. She halved her advertising budget *and* doubled her leads!

Kay's journey was inspiring because I watched her work so hard, mostly alone, to get her results.

Tara: Weight Loss Expert and Video Marketing Consultant

Tara came to one of my events shortly after going through a personal transformation. She had been yo-yo dieting all her life. She would lose weight, keep it off for a short while, but then put it all back on again, gaining a little more weight each time. She finally found a formula that helped her lose weight and keep it off. Key to her success was beating her addiction to chocolate.

What impressed me so much about Tara was, again, how deeply passionate she was about helping others. She couldn't wait to share her knowledge with other people, knowing how many people out there are depressed about their weight. Making money was definitely a by-product of her fulfilling her passion.

Tara was more than ready to speak about her journey and was already posting videos on Facebook. I helped her to find her a much larger audience on Facebook and she went from being watched by 20–30 followers on Facebook Live to over 1,000. With my encouragement she developed a product to sell to her followers. She created both a coaching programme and a short e-book about chocolate addiction. I encouraged her to give away this first e-book for free, explaining how it would help her earn money in the long run because giving away the e-book would help her build a following and would inspire people to trust her. She went on to write a longer book that she was then able to sell at the events she started to run.

I really had to help Tara overcome her fears about creating products. At first she was really unsure about writing books, but

I explained that, once you give people something of *value*, they appreciate it and that you, as the creator, feel that appreciation. I know what it feels like to have enormous appreciation from people; it feels amazing. Once Tara got feedback from her clients and followers, she was inspired to keep going.

Genuine gratitude is a wonderful thing to feel. I love it when my clients get to feel that warmth and gratitude from *their* clients in the way I have felt it from *my* students. It's great to have that shared experience with them.

In an interesting twist to Tara's story, she became so skilled at running Facebook Live campaigns that she created a side business out of it. She now also coaches people on how to create effective content for Facebook Live.

I was delighted that, as well as transforming her original business, Tara became a successful video marketing consultant by accident!

Sophia: Life Coach

Sophia is a qualified life coach. She is based in Edinburgh but is originally from Cyprus. While she had always had huge passion for her business and had worked very hard to promote herself, she had been struggling to make enough money from it. She was finding it difficult to get and keep clients, and she wasn't sure how to set prices that could make the profit she needed in order to invest in and build her business. Many life coaches and therapists have this problem because they only offer one-to-one coaching and repeat business is not always guaranteed. If you are only making £40 per hour, and it takes all your effort to maintain a constant 10–15 clients a week, your income is going to be slim and you are going to have very little money to invest in growing your business.

With any kind of consultancy it is often hard to see how it can be scalable, because a consultant thinks, "It's just me and my expertise, how can I duplicate what I do to scale my business?" Also, just because someone is an expert at helping people on a psychological and behavioural level, it doesn't make them an expert at running a business.

When I first met Sophia, I suggested she attend my marketing programme. Initially she was hesitant because she only had a very limited amount to invest. I explained to her that you have to *invest* money to *make* money, and finally she set aside the money and made the commitment.

On the course that Sophia took, there was a focus on business positioning. I explained to Sophia that even life coaches and therapists need to find a niche offering. For a while, Sophia couldn't think of what her niche could be until, finally, it came to her. She couldn't believe how obvious it was.

Sophia's niche was Cypriot women. In other words, people *exactly* like her. She was a young, attractive, cheerful-looking *woman* and her selling point was that other women wanted to *be like her*. So we made Sophia's branding all about showing her in the most authentic, positive way. This wasn't about a woman dressing up in stylish clothes, or applying lots of make-up, or looking artistic or quirky. Sophia focused on looking natural and – most importantly – *happy* in every picture she took. Her website and Facebook cover images were of *her*, looking relaxed, peaceful and content.

The irony with people like Sophia is that, while they are often very good at helping their clients get their lives on track, they sometimes struggle to get their own lives thriving. The other issue is that the market for therapists and life coaches is completely saturated, and everyone calls themselves an expert. How do you stand out as a true expert when everyone claims to be an expert? Again, this can be addressed by narrowing down a really specific niche. **The one thing no one else can be is *you*.** So the more authentic you can make your branding, the narrower you make your niche. This is why we worked on making Sophia's branding very much a reflection of her genuine self – a young, positive Cypriot woman living in Edinburgh. Once we had that, there was going to be little competition for her.

After securing more clients in the Edinburgh area – mostly women of Greek and Cypriot origin, Sophia took her business to Cyprus and started running events there so that she could work on the "one-to-many" business model instead of the "one-to-one".

By using all the techniques she'd learned on my course that teaches people how to use social media to grow their business, Sophia transformed her digital marketing strategy. She used all the social media tools available and ensured that she got the most for her money.

Sophia learned that the key to successful social media marketing is to find a core, simple message and then keep every single post in line with that theme. She closely applied the "AIDA" formula to every video post she made. She grabbed her audience's **ATTENTION**, and then kept their **INTEREST** in order to help them get the **DESIRE** to take **ACTION**. She also fully embraced the importance of keeping her posts personal, so she is always very authentic in her videos, showing exactly who she is, and instilling everything with her positive personality.

Within five weeks of finishing her course, Sophia contacted me to tell me wonderful news. By using all the tools and strategies that she had learned on the course, such as running ads and doing "Facebook Live" sessions, she had made back every penny she'd spent doing the course! This was fantastic news, especially as she had been so hesitant to spend the money in the first place. It showed her that *you have to invest money to make money*. And invest it *wisely*!

Recently, Sophia's success has been growing exponentially. Although she is still based in Edinburgh, and intends to remain there, she has continued to hold sell-out events in Cyprus and has even been featured on Cypriot TV. She has totally captured the Cypriot market.

Some of Sophia's recent Facebook Live videos have focused on the theme of "happiness". The title of a recent Facebook Live presentation she did was "The 10 habits of incredibly happy people". People tuning into this presentation knew exactly what they were getting. And they got it. They could see proof that Sophia knew exactly what she was talking about because she was a living example of what she was teaching. In every post, there is a clear subliminal message that says, "Let me show you how to be as happy and healthy as I look."

Sophia has continued to hone her message and brand. She totally embraced the importance of getting your positioning (who you are and what you are saying) and your product offering (what you are selling, how you are delivering it and for how much) exactly right. With that core understanding, alongside all the tools she has developed since taking the course, Sophia has continued to enjoy great return on her investment. I am thoroughly enjoying watching her grow and succeed.

Yasmin: Executive Coach

Unlike Sophia, Yasmin did not have an existing business when we first met. She had ideas, but nothing concrete. She also had money to invest. She wanted my help in deciding where to invest her money and time. She wanted to turn her passion for personal development, and for helping and inspiring people, into a business.

Yasmin is originally from Iran. She comes from a traditional family and faced the expectations to be a model mother and take care of her family. But she was also highly educated, holding a PhD, and she wanted to make more of her life.

When Yasmin first came to me for coaching, she was really ready to learn. One of the first concepts she absorbed was the idea of **staying consistent**. Yasmin was fortunate in that she had time; she had passion, but also patience. So many people I meet are almost too impatient. They are desperate to see immediate results and don't understand that building a business can take a long time. They often make mistakes because they are impatient. Yasmin was very lucky in that her business was to be a secondary income, and she had time and money to invest, so she was able to grow slowly and consistently.

Essentially, Yasmin wanted to inspire people to change their lives. I helped her to choose a name and theme for her Instagram account and she decided to focus on posts related to leadership. She knew that leadership was a big theme for her. She then grew her account by posting every day. She ensured her posts were all relevant in content, and she saw her following grow and her engagement increase slowly but consistently. Slowly but surely she grew her Instagram account to 50,000 followers. Her loyal followers loved her content and stayed engaged because they knew they could rely on her to post new content every day. All her posts contained positive and inspiring messages that attracted fans of personal development.

Once Yasmin had achieved over 50,000 followers, an interesting thing started to happen. People started to contact her for advice. At that point her business kicked in, as she was able to charge for that advice. She directed people to her website, understanding that you don't sell anything directly on social media platforms, you *engage* people and then direct them to where they can purchase your product or service. Yasmin is one of the best examples I've ever witnessed of someone monetising their social media following the right way. She accepted that you cannot monetise your social media presence from the start; indeed, it took Yasmin at least six months to grow to the point where she was able to monetise successfully, but she never let up. And it completely paid off!

In a similar way to Sophia, Yasmin found that she got her best results when she targeted her marketing at women just like her – in other words, Iranian women. Her clients are not exclusively from

Iran, but tend to be people who identify with her. She positioned herself as someone who could help women like her and, as with Sophia, it has been extremely successful.

Yasmin is now a well-loved coach to many people, including several celebrities. Her patience and consistency have paid off and it's a pleasure to watch her develop her business further.

I often tell my students the stories of Yasmin and Sophia to show them how, no matter what stage of your business you are at (Sophia was established, Yasmin was not), or how much money you have (Yasmin had a good amount of money to invest, Sophia had limited funds), the same techniques can be applied. The investment, in the end, really comes from *you*. You have to be absolutely clear about your message (which includes your presence/positioning and product/offering). If the message doesn't work, no amount of money will guarantee you a successful business. When you get the message right, everything else will follow.

George: Security Adviser and Mentor

The final success story I want to share with you, briefly, is the story of someone who went through one the most extraordinary personal transformations I have ever seen. Watching someone transform like this is one of the biggest motivators to me.

When I met George, you couldn't imagine a more typical "military guy". He had served in the British Army for many years and had that typical "stiff upper lip". I remember he seemed to talk without any emotion; it seemed as though the ability to connect with people on a really personal level had been stripped out of him by his time in the armed forces. So I suggested he attend my public speaking course. At first he was reluctant. His business was advising companies about their security and how to cope with the threat of terrorist attacks; the idea of speaking in public was completely alien to him and he couldn't see how it would help his business. I knew that, with his knowledge and expertise, he needed to be able to communicate with people in order to sell his services. I also firmly believed that embracing the ability to speak on a stage in public, and let his guard down, would change George's life forever.

I'm happy to say that I was right!

During the course, we all watched George go through a complete personal breakthrough. Immediately after completing the course, George told me that, not only had his business started to take off, but his relationship with his family had also completely changed. This was because, during the public speaking course, George finally let the barriers down. The George I originally met never smiled and seemed fairly unapproachable. The George who left the course was a friendly, communicative, warm person, who smiled and joked in a relaxed way. It really filled me with joy to think that a person who could have gone through the rest of his life being closed and repressed was now not only enjoying a much happier life, but was also inspiring and helping others to do the same.

George ended up developing and expanding his business in order to help people achieve what he had achieved.

Now, while he still reaches out to clients individually and directly, offering them help and advice with their security needs, he also holds workshops and seminars where he gets to speak to and communicate with potential clients in a more personal way. He has positioned himself as an expert in the industry and shares his knowledge on a bigger scale. George has grown to enjoy connecting with people so much that he has developed **his own mentorship programme**, helping people make the kind of breakthrough that transformed his life. He has taken his business to the next level by "humanising" it … in other words, making the whole business about human connection.

Like many people, George needed to find more fulfilment in his working life. Making money is always important, but if you don't get something out of your business, you will not be totally inspired to work at growing it. You have to love what you do and know *why* you are doing it.

Watching people's lives transform, both in their business *and* their personal lives, is *what I love doing and why I do what I do*!

I am extremely proud of all my students, especially as so many have been women who have overcome their lack of self-confidence and become thriving, successful entrepreneurs. In fact, as a result of having worked with so many female entrepreneurs, I was honoured to be chosen by Global Women's Magazine as their "Man of the Year" in 2017 and to be featured on their front cover.

Helping people – women and men – will always be at the core of my business. This is what inspires me and makes me want to get up in the morning!

Final Word: Your Business Story

Ihope two core themes have come across in this book. One is that the secret to my success, and indeed anyone's success, is **helping other people**. When you help others become successful, *you* become successful in the process. Just as, in our families, we pass on knowledge down to the generations that come after us and watch them exceed our achievements, anyone who is successful in business should be motivated to pass on their experiences and advice to the next wave of entrepreneurs.

The other theme, that I hope you have picked up on is that, these days, *anyone* **can be a successful entrepreneur**. The digital revolution means that there are very few barriers to entry. You need a minimal amount of financial investment to start certain businesses. You can even build your own brand through social media and earn money simply by **being you**! Whenever I hear people make excuses for why they haven't started their business yet, or why they haven't been successful, I show them all the ways in which they can overcome their obstacles.

This is why this book is called "Business Hack". Traditional rules and barriers can no longer stop you from making it. There are no more excuses! If you want business success, you can go and get it. No one can stop you but *you*.

I meet so many people, especially those who have been in business for a long time, who are apprehensive about social media, and all the technological developments in cyber communication. There is nothing to fear but lack of knowledge. And there is no excuse for lack knowledge because all the information you need is available to you. These days you have to be a research *fiend*. You can never assume you can stop searching for new information, because the whole world is evolving at an exponential rate.

I said earlier in the book that if there was one message I wanted you to take away from this book it is, **DO NOT UNDERESTIMATE THE POWER OF SOCIAL MEDIA**. That still stands. Embrace social media, use all the tools and learn new tools as soon as they are launched. Through social media, virtually the whole world is at your fingertips. If you don't exploit that, you are not doing yourself justice as a business owner.

I hope you have learned *something* (preferably, a lot!) from this book. Above all else, I hope you have learned this … that *the learning process never stops*. Whatever I have said today may be completely obsolete tomorrow. **The digital world moves at the speed of thought.** Almost as soon as something is conceived of, it can start happening. If you don't keep up, your competitors will get ahead of you. Follow everything and everyone, press every button, stay connected and ride the rollercoaster. You should always be asking questions about what the next development might be.

I never stop learning. Every day I discover something new, that I didn't know before, and I make it my business to learn everything I can about it. I learn from my business associates, I learn from my employees, I learn from my students, I learn from my parents, I learn from my friends, and I learn (a lot!) from my wonderful wife and beautiful daughter. We learn from everyone we come into contact with. Everyone has something to teach you if you keep your eyes and ears open.

So I look forward to hearing about your business journey and learning something from you.

Stay in touch. You know where to find me!

Live as if you were to die tomorrow. Learn as if you were to live forever.

—Mahatma Gandhi

Index

Page references followed by *f* indicate an illustration figure.

.